300 cottage style Decorating Ideas

300 cottage style Decorating Ideas

146

49

155

62

194

272

Cottage Decor 100

58

100 Flea Market Style

100 Garden Style

Cottage DECOR

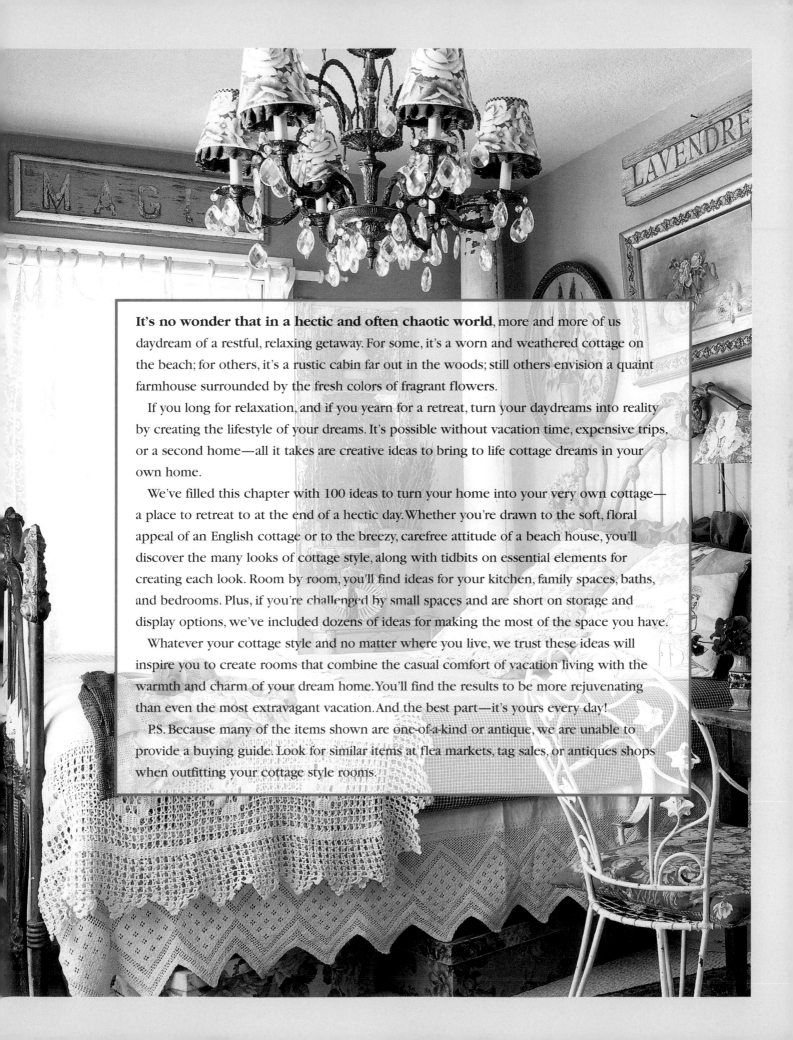

It's no wonder that in a hectic and often chaotic world, more and more of us daydream of a restful, relaxing getaway. For some, it's a worn and weathered cottage on the beach; for others, it's a rustic cabin far out in the woods; still others envision a quaint farmhouse surrounded by the fresh colors of fragrant flowers.

If you long for relaxation, and if you yearn for a retreat, turn your daydreams into reality by creating the lifestyle of your dreams. It's possible without vacation time, expensive trips, or a second home—all it takes are creative ideas to bring to life cottage dreams in your own home.

We've filled this chapter with 100 ideas to turn your home into your very own cottage— a place to retreat to at the end of a hectic day. Whether you're drawn to the soft, floral appeal of an English cottage or to the breezy, carefree attitude of a beach house, you'll discover the many looks of cottage style, along with tidbits on essential elements for creating each look. Room by room, you'll find ideas for your kitchen, family spaces, baths, and bedrooms. Plus, if you're challenged by small spaces and are short on storage and display options, we've included dozens of ideas for making the most of the space you have.

Whatever your cottage style and no matter where you live, we trust these ideas will inspire you to create rooms that combine the casual comfort of vacation living with the warmth and charm of your dream home. You'll find the results to be more rejuvenating than even the most extravagant vacation. And the best part—it's yours every day!

P.S. Because many of the items shown are one-of-a-kind or antique, we are unable to provide a buying guide. Look for similar items at flea markets, tag sales, or antiques shops when outfitting your cottage style rooms.

1

recycled goods

Nostalgic product tins and fruit and veggie cans make nice nooks for whisks, spoons, and more. Just punch or drill a hole in the back near the rim to attach each container with a single screw. Also consider using old colanders in a new way: Convert them into hanging produce bins.

cottage
kitchen

For a cottage kitchen that cooks, you need healthy servings of style and function. Here are a few ingredients to add to your decorating recipe.

2 door dressings

Reveal your cabinetry's softer side by outfitting its doors with fetching fabric. The green-and-white gingham check is used only on the lower portions of the upper cabinets, leaving the upper tiers open for dishware display.

3 wired up

Being cooped up behind chicken wire won't keep this red-and-white toile wallpaper from influencing the rest of this kitchen's character. By adding wire and wallpaper to the faces of this cabinetry, the homeowners gave their bland cooking zone French farmhouse flavor.

4 rollin' along

Thought you'd pinned down the purpose of rolling pins? Think again. These useful kitchen tools also make terrific display items. Available in a variety of colors, materials, and textures, rolling pins can be featured in on- and off-the-wall locations.

5 on the bench

Change your table-setting lineup by calling up a bench. Full of team spirit, benches offer seating for two or more and provide a welcome switch to a chairs-only dining arrangement.

6 carrying on

Let old wooden buckets retire in style. In their after-farm life, wire-bound buckets can be used as happy homes for fruits, vegetables, plants, or fresh flowers.

7 on the edge

What you place on the shelf matters, but what's on the edge matters, too. White porcelain pulls march across the white shelf (*top left*), and a striped-towel border covers up a bare edge (*bottom left*). Other edge-trimming options that add to a shelf's life include antique butter knives, keys, and rulers.

8 curtain call

Fetching tablecloths are a treat for a window as well as a table. Old and new vintage fabrics can be repurposed as curtains simply by folding and tacking them to window trim. ❏

vintageverve

Soaked in punchy patterns from cherries to checks, colorful vintage fabrics are quick fixes for fading rooms. Other colorful collectibles such as Fiestaware and Bristol glass give a kitchen an upbeat attitude and a connection to the past. Here are some helpful hints about fabrics:

Nothing is perfect, nor does it have to be. Flawed fabrics and quilts are often more affordable, and when carefully positioned to show off their best sides, nonperfect items do a great deal to enhance your home's character.

Avoid cutting up salvaged tablecloths and towels. Instead, drape or fold them to preserve their potential to serve you in the future.

In addition to tablecloths, dish towels, picnic napkins, aprons, pillowcases, and embroidery can all do wonders as a window's wardrobe.

Lacy and sheer hankies provide stylishly soft separation without blocking city or suburban views when used as fixed-panel curtains.

9
casual cover-ups

Slip your chairs into something more comfortable. Cozy white-and-blue chair covers and cushions are the stars of this romantic breakfast setting. Hanging hats and a parade of pitchers are cast in supporting roles along the wall and on the windowsill.

focus on
family

Personable and practical, cottage style is well-suited to a home's public spaces. Soft fabrics, cozy chairs, and fetching finds create inviting rooms that welcome family and friends.

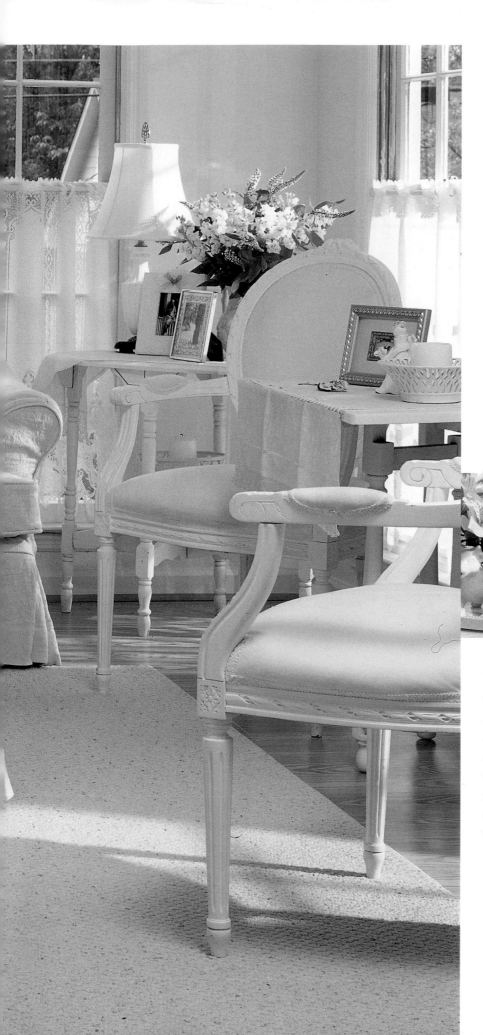

10

white wonders

White—with its many shades—is the quintessential color for all cottage styles, except camp. In addition to being crisp and clean, white has a softer side that makes rooms feel warm and inviting. In this living room, snowy hues blanket an armoire, cushy chairs, and tattered tables to create an overall sense of welcome.

bright blends 11

Along the shore or near a city street, a cottage with beach styling boasts cheerful colors and punchy patterns. Upbeat blues, crisp whites, and radiant reds anchor this sitting room's color scheme, which calls for collaboration among fruity and floral patterns, stripes, checks, and nautical notions. Walls with beaded board at half-mast further underscore this room's nautical nature.

12

collectible cues

Collections are a great place to start when it comes to picking a palette for your living space. Vibrant blue-and-white vases and glassware dictate the color direction for this sophisticated living space.

13 it's a (tin) wrap

Whitewashed tin tiles make fun and fabulous frames for small and sizable mirrors alike. Beyond frames, tin tiles—new or old, painted or plain—can be used to create pretty plant holders, tabletops, ceilings, backsplashes, and more.

14 earning stripes

When you pick out a primary pattern for a large furniture piece, seek out opportunities to repeat the motif in smaller and midsize doses for the sake of balance and cohesive styling. In this space, an armoire establishes a striped scheme that is echoed by the sofa pillows and fireplace built-ins. ❏

15 tuck and fold

Put old shelving units to work in new ways. This weathered and worn multilevel rack squeezes in accessible storage space for gotta-have goods. Though its primary purpose is functional, the unit also serves to present everyday items in an eye-catching manner.

bath
spaces

To fulfill their potential, bathrooms often need a boost. Showering a bath with snappy storage components is what makes a brush-and-wash room both good-looking and hardworking.

16

16 à la carte

Islands aren't just for kitchen setups. If you have room and could use more stow-away space, you can roll in a metal cart to serve as your bath's central storage oasis. Another simple storage solution: hanging metal wire bins on the wall.

17 exposed

Open up! Removing cabinet doors creates a sense of spaciousness in a tight bath. Here the doorless beaded-board built-ins store and showcase bath essentials such as toiletries, towels, and decorative knickknacks.

18 bath essentials

Like any table and chair, this minty green furniture is set to serve, this time in the bath. The spoke-back chair and tiny table supplement this cottage bath with storage space for towels and toiletries. Because baths and powder rooms usually have shoebox-size dimensions, you'll want to seek out slimmer tables and smaller chairs to serve your bath storage needs. To ensure a perfect fit, measure your space before heading out to shop.

19 fairest of them all

Decorating with mirrors is an idea worthy of reflection. Mirrors add depth and dimension to smaller-size baths and enhance the sense of light. For an eclectic elegance, mix and match mirrors of different sizes, shapes, and colors.

20

20 washed up

Converting a dresser into a sink station gives family heirlooms new function and brings furniture styling to the bath. Even though dressers retrofitted for plumbing forfeit maximum storage space, there's still room inside the reconfigured drawers for linens and more.

21 basket case

Awash in fresh white and country character, this bath supplements built-in storage with open-air options. Filled with towels, toilet tissue, and other stock items, baskets provide storage and impart beauty with their wonderful weaves. Plus, their varied sizes, shapes, and colors make them an easy addition to any bath.

22 plain and tall

Wrought with possibilities, this iron CD tower plays well in a powder room or bath. The sleek unit squeezes vertical storage potential into an empty corner and houses fun and functional bath items alike. ❏

"There is no need to go to India or anywhere else to find peace.... You will find that deep place of silence right in your room, your garden, or even your bathtub."

—Elisabeth Kubler-Ross

23

fence sense

Need a headboard? Fencing is a quick and easy bedside solution. Well-aligned and white, these pickets line up to create a wonderful heading for a bed. Offering visual warmth, color, and comfort, quilts stacked and stored at the foot of the bed are a classically cottage touch.

resting
places

Bedrooms are sanctuaries for *sweet dreams and style statements.* Blanket your sleeping spaces with soft fabrics and personal touches to create a restful retreat.

24

purple passion

A marvelous mix of textures, trinkets, and winsome purple walls makes this sleeping setup restful and romantic. Weathered shutters, lacy cover-ups, signs, and flowery fare reinforce the bedroom's sweet charm.

25

natural selections

The camp side of cottage style embraces nature's best and makes it feel cozy. Forest green fabrics partner with a cut-log bed frame to give this bedroom its rustic bent.

setting up camp

Whether you're living within the city limits or outside them, you can pack your living quarters with this rustic, Earth-friendly look. Here are some tips on how to domesticate the wilderness for the sake of cottage's camp style.

Be a sport: Active endeavors are essential to surviving life in the wild, and thus sporting supplies are essential to this style. Hunting, fishing, camping, and skiing gear and signs give walls sporty splendor.

Woodsy wonders: Even if it could, camp style wouldn't chuck wood. Rather, this look puts wood to work. Logs, twigs, and bark make textural touches for furniture, walls, and accessories.

Warm and weighty themes: The camp palette includes deep greens, reds, and blues, as well as softer shades such as mossy greens, bark browns, and river-rock grays. Patterns also have their place. Chunky stripes, rich plaids, and buffalo checks are well-suited to homes situated along a mountain pass.

26
special treatment

Painted patterns can punch up any room. The window wall in this bedroom sports a yellow coat of paint, stencil patterns, and a white ribbon of hooks for hanging displays. The eye-catching flooring features a two-tone yellow checkerboard pattern. Be selective about which surfaces get special treatment. Too many patterns in too many places overwhelm the eye.

27 fairy-tale fabrics

To make your sleeping beauty more dreamy, consider dressing up her bed. Sheathed by a vintage-style chenille coverlet and a sprinkling of embroidered pillows, this bed exhibits understated charm. A sheer canopy tops off the soft setup. This princesslike component can be made with a white scarf sconce and six yards of sheer fabric.

28 painted pretty

Bring a bedroom to life with a pretty paint treatment. This space is a bounty of pink pansy and gladiola blooms, post-top birdhouses, and a white picket fence. When choosing a motif or stencil pattern, try to select a style or pattern and colors that offer timeless, tireless appeal. ❏

"The cool kindliness of sheets, that soon smooth away trouble; and the rough male kiss of blankets."

—Rupert Brooke

29

lullaby look

A soft palette, cushioned rockers, and a window box contribute soothing comfort to this growing environment. Always ready for storytime, a yellow chenille bunny brings life to one rock-a-bye rocker.

kid-friendly

Easygoing and inviting, the cottage look lets you build a decorating style that caters to the tastes of a home's younger residents.

bold and bright

A cross between beach and camp styles, this boy's bedroom boasts vivid quilts and blankets that offer visual and physical comfort. Young creativity is captured in the frames over the beds, and a collection of toy cars and trucks drives home the idea that boys will always be boys when it comes to their toys and treasures.

fabric frolic

Balance is key to a fashionably fit home. Use these guidelines to partner plain and patterned fabrics for indoor and outdoor fare.

Start by choosing a primary pattern. This pattern can be used in a wall covering, fabric, area rug, or bedspread. This element should include all of the colors you want to use in the space. (The pattern's more prominent hues will guide your picks for paint colors and accessories.)

One size doesn't fit all. A healthy mix of small, medium, and large motifs will help maintain visual balance. For example, blend bold checks with at least two different-size motifs, such as a petite plaid and a medium floral print.

To give your eyes a place to rest, use solid or neutral colors for flooring and furniture. A solid- or neutral-color sofa is a strong anchor that allows for greater flexibility should you opt to alter a room's mood in the future.

31

ENGLISH
WATCH MAKER

31 boy's life

A mix of bed dressings and under-bed baskets establishes cottage character. Other identifiable components include an antique fan, sporty rowing oars, and a jar of marbles. A propeller on top of a headboard offers a touch of whimsy.

32 floral frenzy

Flowery fabrics and floor and wall coverings give this young girl's room a feminine flourish with English cottage roots. An ensemble of fabric and ribbon gives the closet door renewed purpose as a display for pictures and postcards.

33 crib-side couture

Instead of simply putting clothes on, put them on display. Sweet gowns, small dresses, and ballerina wear dangle from plush hangers and wooden hooks to impart girlish delight.

34 boy toys

These antique toys play well with others. Mingling among books, jackets, and a baseball mitt, the old toys show that boys, like girls, just want to have fun. ❏

35

bench marks

Beyond the ballpark, benches can benefit from winning views. Two tiny benches give this window treatment some ground-level glory with their floral fabric topping. They can also do duty as petite perches for small plants that need to be within the sweep of sun rays.

chairs, benches, & tables

Chairs, benches, and tables can hold more stylistic weight than you think. Let these functional furnishings add flights of fancy to your home.

36 clear and clever

Rotund glass urns bear a stock glass tabletop to create a congenial coffee table. Consider terra-cotta pots or cast concrete urns as other supportive substitutes.

37 discarded delights

You don't have to keep cabinetry boxed in. Topped with a piece of wood, painted, and put on a pedestal, two discarded cabinet drawers are used to create a great end table. This drawer duo is an ideal place to stash catalogs and remote controls.

38

38 photo finish

Even with a foot, a bed can't walk; but the right edge-of-bed treatment gives a bed style it can stand on. A queen-size bench accents this sleeping beauty, offering ample landing space for favorite photos and keepsakes.

39 super seats

Style-supplementing and service-oriented seats are no strangers to cottage style. Offering support for people, plants, and more, chairs that feature eye-catching curves, comfy cushions, and interesting materials deserve floor space. ❏

39

"I had three chairs
in my house;
one for solitude,
two for friendship,
three for society."

— Henry David Thoreau

40
shaker style

Salt-and-peppered out, these vintage shakers have new life as sanctuaries for small-stem flowers. (You can use an awl to enlarge the shaker holes.) After arranging your blooms, position flowers where they can catch some rays.

storage
&display

Must-have storage and optional displays are two easy ways to incorporate cottage style components into your living spaces. These examples show you how.

41

41 iron supplements

Recast as wall hangings, cast-iron stove-top grills
are an example of functional elements that make fun
accessories. These hot-off-the-grill components
create cool on-the-wall combinations with their
varied designs.

42 bottled beauty

Olive oil and vinegar bottles are vases in waiting. Once
the oil and vinegar are gone, wash the bottles and
dress them in ribbons, raffia, or faux or dried flowers,
and then place fresh-cut blooms inside.

43

43 pet project

To make spaces personal, decorate with a few of your favorite things. Here dog lovers express their affection for furry friends with a crop of black-and-white puppy photos positioned on their living room shelves.

44 memory jarring

Nestle photos inside a large jar you want to use for storage, and slip a smaller-size jar inside to hold the photos in place and corral pencils, paintbrushes, and other desktop essentials.

45 tea times

An old tea tray takes on a new job as a photo frame. Find a tray with glass, or retrofit a glassless frame, and then add handles to opposite edges.

faces and places

Beyond plastic sleeves in leather wallets and family albums, photographs have a place in the lives of cottage dwellers. Taking time to organize favorite photographs in new and innovative ways helps you enhance your decor and celebrate your personal history on a daily basis. An old tea tray with a glass insert is a great way to serve up a favorite photograph, as is displaying a handful of images on a dashing band of ribbon. Outfitting old windows or an old corkboard with a plain or fancy grid presents images in a candid fashion. Clustering images of friendly faces and favorite places on a table is fun for guests. Simply arrange photos, and cover the table with a fitted pane of glass. Postcards and cherished poems and letters are also great candidates for these treatments.

46

photogenic

With a fitted piece of glass, you can convert a
coffee table into a display for your most
memorable Kodak moments, cherished
postcards, or even remnants from your
flower garden. This showcase is easily reborn
to suit changing seasons or tastes.

47 a window through time

This salvaged window gives a voice to the past with its display of black-and-white and sepia prints. An easy weave of rope—or ribbon, if you prefer—makes this picturesque exhibition possible.

48 starring role

Let shapely artifacts such as starfish help you spotlight photographic memories of summers spent at the beach. Blue-and-white fabric builds the bridge between the starry sea notions and picture frames.

49 backing it up

Give blank built-ins a lesson in style by lining the back surfaces with pages from an old textbook. In keeping with the natural theme found in the background text, these shelves showcase pinecones, acorns, shells, and other earthy elements.

shell-bound

Summer's best souvenirs are found by the seashore. To keep memories of sea sojourns in sight, consider clustering shells around pillar candles or placing them on shelves or tables or into clear glass vases. Pretty pebbles, starfish, and sand dollars can also be used to revitalize an old frame or mirror. You can make beach elements a more permanent part of your home decor by embedding them in backsplashes, countertops, or patio sidewalks. Here are some shell collecting tips:

The best time to hit the beach for shell shopping is at low tide or after a big storm.

Some shells change color after they dry. To restore gloss and color, wipe them down with mineral oil or baby oil, or use an acrylic spray.

To create chalky white shells, mix 1 quart of water with 1 cup of bleach. Soak shells 30 minutes, and then let them dry in the sunshine.

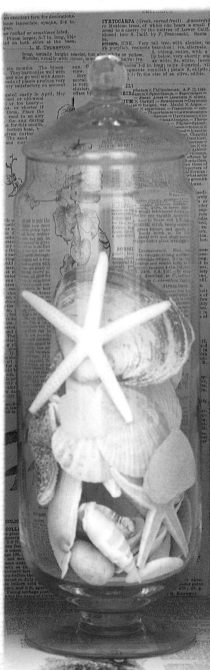

50 knob appeal

Architectural-salvage fixtures such as shower handles make super spots for dangling wet towels and bath robes. Vintage doorknobs with handsome finishes or glass figures are also good hang-ups.

51 hooked up

Consider bringing hefty hook hardware in from the stable. This black-iron beauty provides a sturdy hangout for light and heavy fare alike.

52 fork lift

A drill, a single nail, and pretty ribbon transform a functional fork into a sharp-looking support for a photo frame. Be sure to find a frame light enough for a vintage fork to support.

53 arch support

By adding a handful of age-old hooks, a rustic salvage piece with swirly motifs becomes a hang-up for pajamas or freshly ironed day wear.

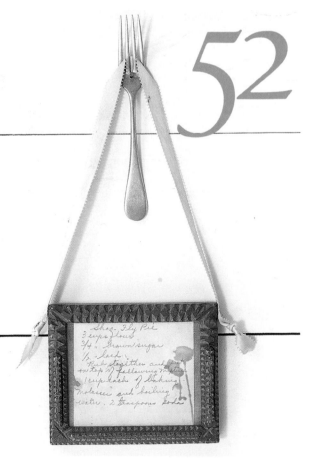

53

54 finial fun

Homemade rods and finials are fanciful and fun.
Group a white curtain with rope hooks, old crystal
doorknobs, and a chunky bamboo stick to build a
simply charming window treatment.

55 metal jacket

A curvaceous metal swag wraps around the shoulders
of this farmhouse window. Affixed with nails, the
silvery treatment offers spirit and shine.

56 oh so twiggy

With glue and a nail gun, a natural selection of willow
branches and pinecones changes ordinary bifold
doors into a winning display of camp cottage style.

56

57 tick tock

Brighten dreary areas with cherished collections. Topped with a slice of wood, this radiator makes a great roosting place for a clock collection and a family of snow-color pitchers.

58 shoe-in

Fancy antique footwear walks the walk of quick-and-easy decorating. This hanging cupboard with aged edges lets these old baby shoes put their best foot forward.

59 boxing lessons

Hats off to hatboxes! Stack these lovely boxes on shelves, or position them at floor level. These flowery containers flourish just about anywhere and can be bought for their good looks or for their storage potential.

60 fab frame

Picture this: An old photo frame can easily be converted into a fetching vanity tray. Simply outfit an old frame with a matching-size mirror, and place your beauty supplies inside.

61 boxed in

Window boxes don't have to hibernate during winter months. Colored glass bottles and flickering candles make classy cold-season substitutes for spring and summer blooms.

62 storage ajar

Pasta, sugar, flour, and other cooking staples show their true colors when stored in clear glass kitchen jars. In addition to their stunning, down-home simplicity, old or new jars let you gauge what supplies need replenishing.

63 sign language

Signs, signs, everywhere there's signs. Let old-time sign boards have their say in rooms for which their messages are appropriate.

64 pail faces

Formerly used to trap and transport tree sap, these buckets now serve as savory additions to indoor decor. Hang buckets on the wall for home-supply storage, or consider repurposing pails to display flowers on walls or at floor level. ❏

65

you've got game

Checkmate! But in this case, everyone who plays is a winner. This stairway offers a friendly and noncompetitive environment for a game-board collection.

delectable
collectibles

Collectibles catch the eye and capture the heart. These ideas show you how to fit your favorite things into everyday spaces.

66 dishing out blues

In addition to featuring a tabletop quilt, this setting offers a delicious collection of blue transferware. Coloring the walls, filling shelves, and servicing the table, these dishes add a desirable blue mood to any cottage-sensitive dining space.

patchwork perks

Quilts are one of cottage style's unquestionable comforts. Hanging on the wall, topping a table, or backing up a couch, quilts bring visual and physical warmth and add punchy color to a room. On-the-wall locations are safe places for quilts you want to keep in mint condition. For high-traffic and worry zones, such as sofas and tabletops, it's best to assign quilts that are already showing signs of age.

67

"America is not like a blanket—one piece of unbroken cloth, the same color, the same texture, the same size. America is more like a quilt—many patches, many pieces, many colors, many sizes, all woven and held together by a common thread."

—Jesse Jackson

68

decor by number (and letter)

An affinity for letters and numbers can result in a snappy decorative solution. Use initials or favorite numbers to cast simple shapes onto home elements such as chairs, picture frames, storage sacks, mirrors, buckets, lamp shades, dishes, and platters.

69

fan-atical

Exhibiting fantastic form, these blowers bring a breeze of style to your shelves. When shopping for fans, diversify your collection by seeking models of varying size, shape, color, and blade design. A bonus: If they're broken, you don't have to fix them; your purchases can be based on good looks alone.

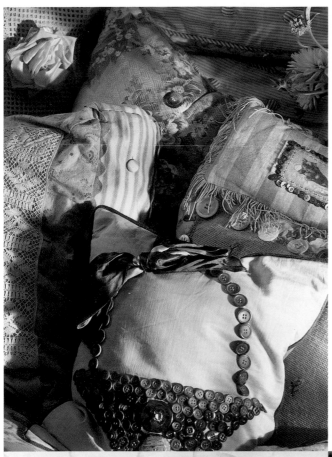

70
pillow punch

Made from vintage yardage or tablecloths, sewn with love, and decked out in fringe, buttons, and lace, pillows offer easy access to the cottage look. Count on pillows to perk up plain surfaces, change the face of a room, or soften wooden furniture with their cushy charm.

71 tender treasures

Old linens can be fragile, but that need not hamper their decorating performance. Antique heirlooms are able accents for furniture such as this outdoor table. It's best to use slightly worn pieces in exterior settings.

72 piled and pretty

Reserve mint-condition materials for indoor staging. Wrap collections of posh fabrics in ravishing ribbons and bows, and leave them out for all to see rather than tucking them away in a linen closet.

73 hanky hang-ups

Grandpa's hanky finds a home outside his pocket. A monogrammed handkerchief spreads out to create a window treatment, offering a bit of privacy without limiting light. ❏

flower power

Plant breeder Luther Burbank once said, "Flowers always make people better, happier, and more helpful; they are sunshine, food, and medicine to the soul." Burbank's words do a fine job of explaining why flowers will forever be a favorite element of cottage style. Held by pots, vases, or farm-style buckets, these natural beauties bring inside spaces to life with their fresh colors and sweet scents. Flowers also make fetching fillers on cake tops and cards. But even when winter has had its way with the garden and fresh flowers are few, flowers endure the seasons by flourishing in fabrics, on frames, and on other surfaces, such as walls, floors, rugs, and carpets with patterns that are embroidered, stenciled, or painted. It's in these forms that flowers survive the seasons and offer lasting beauty.

74

main frames

Overlapping picture frames and objects of
other shapes—a round trivet, a triangular
bracket, candlesticks, and a lone newel
post—form an artistic arrangement against
a sunny hearth wall.

salvaged treasures

It's true: Secondhand objects make first-rate accessories. Embellish your present setting with artifacts salvaged from the past.

75 bold moldings

Soaked in color, this sink station showcases reclaimed moldings in a vertical side-by-side arrangement. The assembled moldings form a rainbow apron for the washbasin and cheerful cabinet doors.

76 firm plantings

Positioned in a sun-friendly spot, this pretty architectural post doubles as a plant shelter for petite violets or other potted plantings.

75

77

77 able table

Notions like this weighty column put a neoclassical twist on this cottage style room. The table can be used to serve freshly brewed coffee or tea or to show off garden-fresh delights.

78 lamp post

Put an old baluster to work as a light-giving accessory. The post's aged appearance pairs wonderfully with a bead-trimmed shade covered in pale pink and green blooms.

79 screen splendor

Fencing from a Charleston walkway stokes the character of this fireplace facade. Another screen idea: Use a section of an old iron gate. During the months when your hearth is without fire, hook together vintage wooden shutters like an accordion to form an eye-catching warm-weather screen.

pretty prop

The right salvage piece can perform wonderfully in a
supporting role. Adding two white, weathered corbels
underneath the countertop imparts instant age to this
kitchen island. Everything else—chunky white
moldings, beaded-board cabinetry, retro bar stools,
and a classic checkerboard floor—works to secure the
kitchen's cottage roots. ❑

fanciful finds

For creative minds, someone else's junk is promising material for upcoming projects. Remnants of fallen homes and buildings are often used to bring a breath of fresh flair to cottage quarters. In fact, a single piece, such as a sturdy vintage fireplace surround, can be used as the cornerstone of a room's decorating style. Or a batch of architectural scraps can be used to unite a room thematically—Victorian garden accents, corbels, or moldings. Here are other ideas for salvage-seekers:

Wall-mount corbels and top them with glass for a slim serving table or a hallway display.

Convert leaded- or stained-glass windows into eye-catching coffee tables by giving them legs.

Use a pair of shutters to frame interior windows, or single one out as a storage and display rack for photos, letters, and bills.

Turn a newel post from an antique staircase into a sturdy plant stand.

Create a floor screen fashioned from antique doors hinged together to dress up a corner or softly separate spaces.

Transform old doors or fanciful gates into artsy architectural headboards.

Gingerbread trim, corbels, and balusters can be used to beautify bare walls or floor space around the hearth.

81

table setting

Plant a worn-but-pretty potting table in
your hallway as a home for green plants,
display items, or handbags and mail. A
small flock of sandpipers in the transom
over the doorway helps the outdoorsy
decor take flight.

bring the
outdoors in

To enjoy the great outdoors the whole year through, enlist natural objects and exterior embellishments to outfit interior spaces.

82

83

82 wired-up props

Put up a white wire shelf to handle interior window-box duties—housing greenery potted in pastel-color containers that can be enjoyed all year long.

83 screen scene

Give tired screen doors a wake-up call. The product of a fresh paint job and some tender loving creativity, this dreamy screen door serves as a snazzy and subtle separation between interior living spaces.

84

84 easy being green

A green theme and exterior elements—Adirondack chairs, garden signage, and watering cans—combine to create an indoor sitting room with outdoor sensibilities.

85 for the birds

Birdhouses come in many colors, sizes, and roof slopes and can be tucked into interior spaces just as easily as in the backyard.

86 picket lines

Flanked by star-and-moon shutters, this picket gate makes a whimsical focal point for a living room wall. The shutters and gate echo the yellow and green found in the fabrics and on other items throughout the space.

"In all things
of nature
there is
something
of the
marvelous."

—Aristotle

85

87
framed fancy

Green-thumbed homeowners turned their album of dried flowers into a wonderful wall of art with clean-lined photo frames. Create a display whose roots are in your own backyard: Gather and dry flowers from your garden to create a similar arrangement.

88 lattice topping

Lattice makes a lovely ceiling treatment for rooms with an outdoor connection. In a cedar wood color, as shown, or under a coat of white paint, lattice reminds indoor spaces of their outdoor roots and gives them garden-style texture.

89 outside-in

White Adirondack furnishings establish a light and breezy outdoor feel in this farmhouse living room. Navy-stripe pillows and cushions let this wooden furniture show a softer side. ❏

opening up

Like windows, doors deserve special treatment. Louvered shutter doors—even when they are always open—add historical flavor to indoor-outdoor pass-throughs.

stepping
out

Don't keep cottage style cooped up; let it wander into your garden or backyard, where it is free to mingle with Mother Nature.

91 veggie bouquets

Fortify your dining area with healthy centerpieces. Heads of cauliflower are fresh and fetching table toppers for this terrace room. Outdoor chairs sport elegant slipcovers for a special occasion.

92 decked out

Curtains with furniture motifs softly sweep this lattice-lined deck. Thanks to these fabric treatments, a mealtime buffet gains a sense of intimacy within the large garden.

93

94

93 hanging around

This camp-cottage porch stays rooted in nature with its branch-made chair and table. A rich blue-and-white pillow and seat cushion contribute a bit of contrast to the woodsy browns. Coaxed out of the kitchen, an ironware tub fills a need for wall decor.

94 easy chairs

Bistro chairs, often featured in Impressionist paintings, were designed to be folded and moved easily between indoor and outdoor spaces. Painted in bright hues, these chairs make cheerful additions to garden rooms.

95 rear window

Outdoor structures give patios architectural allure. This windowed pergola serves as a barrier while preserving a view of the horizon and neighboring field.

"Gardens and flowers have a way of bringing people together, drawing them from their homes."

—Clare Ansberry

95

> **"I hope that while so many people are out smelling the flowers, someone is taking the time to plant some."**
>
> —Herbert Rappaport

96 fabric softener

Fabric visually softens outdoor furniture. Plus, it gives it country charm that's well-suited to an outdoor gathering or garden tea. This bench wears a loose-fitting sheath made of vintage pink floral fabric. The cover is held on by fabric ties, which keep it in place on windy days and make it easy to remove in the event of rain.

porch perfection

A glass of lemonade, a cozy chair, the scent of the garden or the sea—these are the things that make a perfect porch. Bring cottage style comfort to your outdoor retreat with these tips.

Deck the walls: Fill the exterior walls as you would those of any indoor space. A picture or two, old signs, hanging planters, or architectural salvage pieces give a porch home-style appeal.

Super seating: Wicker, metal, or wooden chairs, sofas, and chaise longues make ideal perches for porches. When picking fabrics for cushions, choose outdoor materials that resist fading and stand up to wind, rain, and unexpected spills.

Room for dining: Include a table or two. Dining outdoors is a wonderful way to enjoy nature during warm months.

Green garnishes: Populate your porch with plantings. Hanging plants, plant stands, and pretty pots bring seating setups to life.

97

tool time

Dig in! Tools for pruning , planting, and weeding cultivate style in your outdoor spaces as well as your garden beds. The handy implements spruce up a shed or garage wall and remain accessible for any grassroots tasks that might come up.

98 hook-ups

This porch's privacy stems from its striped curtains, sewn from durable awning fabric. The curtains have rings that allow them to be hung from hooks. This outdoor room's cottage posture is furthered by a mix of wicker furniture and softly patterned pillows and cushions.

99

100

99 winsome window

Pairing a salvaged window with a boxy beaded-board base produces an environmentally friendly treasure. This wonderful window box is worthy of space on the side of your garage or shed.

100 simply swinging

Relax. Hammocks are the perfect place for lounging, reading, or sneaking in some shut-eye under the watch of the sun. Instead of going with a ho-hum hammock, find one with cottage flair and supplement it with a colorfully patterned pillow. ❏

flea market STYLE

Flea market fanatics are a special breed—energetic, creative, and optimistic.
You trek miles out of your way to look at old stuff displayed in pastures. You plan vacations to include markets in other parts of the country. You brake for tag sales, junk stores, antiques malls, thrift shops, and sometimes (although you won't admit it), you even head for the piles your neighbors leave on the curb for trash day.

But your true genius lies not in the attaining but in the transforming. Anyone can put fresh flowers in an antique pitcher. You, on the other hand, buy an old trophy and use it to hold flatware. A pile of battered leather suitcases becomes a coffee table. A rusted garden gate makes a striking headboard. The world is a treasure trove of one-of-a-kind items that express your personal decorating style with wit, character, and creativity.

This chapter is a tribute to flea market fans everywhere. You'll find 100 fresh, creative, and mostly low-cost ways of giving your latest finds new functions. Check out "Inspirations for Every Room" (*page 104*) to see what you can do with your kitchens, baths, bedrooms, living spaces, and outdoor areas. Additional sections offer ideas on working with fabric (*page 140*), furniture (*page 146*), and metal (*page 154*). Then turn to *page 160* to begin touring entire homes that showcase a range of styles—from urban and cottage to new country and Colonial—all guaranteed to charge your creative juices.

We hope our ideas inspire you to look at your favorite antique and secondhand objects with a fresh eye for how they can be used in your home. You'll see that the process can be just as much fun as the results.

P.S. Since all of the items pictured are one-of-a-kind, we hope you will understand why we aren't able to provide a buying guide. Our goal is to inspire you to create your own unique style. Happy shopping!

inspirations
for every room

You've already mastered the art of finding bargains at a flea market. But how can you bring these treasures into your house without disturbing the existing decorating scheme? Browse through these pages for inspiration. You'll see how ordinary folks bring flea market finds into their homes with striking results.

The number one rule of flea market decorating: Nothing should be a perfect match. Case in point: The eight chairs that surround this handsome 14-foot table show a glorious disdain for replication. In fact, each family member bought his or her own chair at a flea market. This grouping works because the other design elements in the room are kept simple.

kitchens and eating areas

Flea market treasures belong in the rooms where you share meals and laughter with friends and family. Whether they work hard, such as a farm basin reincarnated as a sink, or they serve as eye candy, as in whisk brooms impersonating a window valance, these well-worn and much-loved items will instantly feel like old favorites.

2

Wicker Always Works These wicker chairs look just as fashionable paired with a glass-topped table in a formal dining room as they do on a porch or patio. Vintage lace tablecloths float from the windows, adding a feminine flair.

Fifties Throwback With their sleek curves and large capacity, ranges from the 1950s are hot. This one was found for $50 at a garage sale and refurbished for everyday use. The marble shelves and decorative metal brackets—also flea market rescues—add convenient storage.

4. Signs of the Time Find old advertisements in a rainbow of colors and a medley of sizes. These signs suit this Colonial kitchen, imparting the look of an old general store (minus the penny candy). A Douglas fir table—a $40 find at a salvage yard—once served the Stanford University geology department. With a fresh top, it now serves a family.

5. Fresh from the Farm You may not think that a scuffed farm table has any use left, but this one fits in perfectly as a kitchen island—and it's just the right height for chopping vegetables or mixing cookie dough. Chairs and stools (cheap chic if you don't mind that they don't match) are ready for sit-down snacks.

6. Old Wood for New Cabinets Wood recycling is a trend that complements flea market style. The doors of these lower cabinets are constructed of old pine, and the tin inserts (rescued from a dilapidated pie safe) conceal a small refrigerator, an ice maker, and a wine cooler. The copper sink is from an antiques fair.

7. Lofty Ideas Architectural salvage transforms one wall of this modern loft into a kitchen with character. Custom-made cabinets house windows rescued from a razed building. For countertop lighting, tin shades, purchased for a dollar each, are fashioned into pendant lights by adding electrical cable, sockets, and bulbs.

8. A Clean Sweep Flea market shoppers have an ability to see beauty and value in everyday items. At the window in this breakfast room, whisk brooms in varying shades and sizes stand in for a valance. And an old pie safe is put to good use by displaying spongeware and Red Wing pottery.

Simple as Pie Vintage metal pie plates decorate an awkward and empty space in this pine-paneled kitchen. Grouped on the wall, they become a work of art that suits the 1920s white-enameled stove below. Now restored to working order, the stove proudly serves as this country kitchen's centerpiece. ❏

living spaces

Want to *really* show off your vintage treasures? Put them in rooms where the whole

crew congregates—where family and friends gather for parties and get-togethers.

See how these salvaged pieces fit into the following living spaces and practically

become members of the family.

Fireplace Finesse Old window shutters painted in fresh colors stand at attention in front of the fireplace. This type of arrangement is best for filling an otherwise black hole during warmer months.

11 **Boot Hill** Old ladders still have a lot of use left in them—even if they're not as sturdy as they used to be. Offering a rustic counterpoint to a stately cherry armoire, this ladder displays well-worn leather cowboy boots marching up its rungs.

13

Grate Table Want to know a salvage secret? Building a piece of wood furniture around a salvaged item is a smart and creative way to incorporate bargains into your home. Here, an old metal heating grate nestles in a wooden frame topped with glass, *left* and *below*, and functions as a coffee table in this family room.

12. Room Punctuation Though a bit pricey, large salvaged pieces pack an architectural punch that smaller items can't. Even in a bland or new house, this substantial wooden column, which bears the marks of age, adds a bold exclamation point to a comfortable family room.

14

Rising Stars Sturdy metal stars—inexpensive and widely available at flea markets and antiques stores—make simple but striking window decorations, especially when the cornices are short and simple. You'll enjoy mixing and matching these celestial treasures in metal finishes that are painted, rusted, or bare.

15

Beyond the Box (Springs)
Looking at vintage items with
a fresh eye can result in unexpected
beauty. In this room, an old woven
mattress support made of wooden
splints becomes a piece of primitive art.

16

Mix Master Proof that all kinds of styles can play well together, this living room sports curtains made from parachutes (purchased at an army surplus store), old-fashioned bowling pins, and a 19th-century trunk topped with kilim pillows and surrounded by lamps with sculptural paper shades.

17 **Window Wall** Windows salvaged from an office building are joined with screws and make a wall dividing the living area from the bedroom. Stacked suitcases offer scads of storage for little-used items and off-season clothing.

Urban/Industrial Style

Think downtown, big-city, loftlike spaces with sky-high ceilings, exposed brick, and heating ducts, and torrents of sunlight pouring through windows that line the walls. That's urban/industrial style.

At flea markets, watch for metal items that may have had an industrial or commercial use, including office furniture, hospital gurneys, store fixtures, and pillars. Partner your architectural salvages with sleek, clean-lined furnishings and the color black, which adds depth and definition.

Patterns should be kept to a minimum—allowing color and texture to be the focal points of the room. Fabrics are not fancy, but they still command attention. Consider using metallic-red linens or making a window treatment from an old parachute.

Finish the look with a gum-ball machine and other quirky accessories. ❏

bedrooms

Of all the rooms in the house, the bedroom shelters us the most. It's private and personal, and it wards off outside forces that may worry or distress us. Incorporating vintage fabrics and furnishings—items that nurtured others before us—will make this retreat even more comforting and cozy.

18

Vintage-Fabric Frenzy You can't go wrong mixing mellow vintage fabrics. This ultra-feminine bed cuddles in layers of flea market linens in florals and lace. As a clever bed-skirt substitute, a pair of old bedspreads is placed between the mattress and box spring and hangs to the floor. The café curtains, also made of timeworn fabric, provide privacy while allowing light to permeate the room.

Layers of Charm Embellish pillows and curtains with your favorite flea market fabrics, trims, and buttons—it's a great way to display your creativity. Some of the pillows utilize mother-of-pearl buttons and scraps of fabric from a wedding dress belonging to the homeowner's grandmother. And, proving that expensive style doesn't have to cost much, a Victorian-era chair (purchased for $5) furnishes the room with romance.

20. Built Around Quilts Quilt collectors know that not every sample is suitable for display in its entirety. If you get hold of a damaged or incomplete quilt, consider using it as a bed coverlet or a wall hanging. Framing a quilt block utilizes an otherwise unusable scrap of fabric and adds color to an empty space on the wall. Quilt blocks also make charming pillow shams, especially when the colors accentuate elements in the room's upholstery or bedding.

21. Crowning Touch With its curved shape and triangular panes, this wall-hung window adds a dramatic touch to a painted iron-and-brass headboard. Old-fashioned quilts—stacked on a bench—provide a soft counterpoint to the other hard surfaces. Displays such as these are perfect for using quilts that have been damaged or stained. Fold them just right, and no one will ever know.

22. Linens and Lace Hutches aren't just for dining rooms or kitchens. A bedroom can benefit from their storage potential just as much as other rooms do. Here, feminine lace edges the shelves of an old hutch, which displays fluffy blankets, crisp sheets, and white pottery. A well-ridden rocking horse perches on top and adds a touch of whimsy.

23. Basket Case For a sophisticated, clean look, stick with a tone-on-tone palette and then add texture. This soothing bedroom features white in all its glory—crisp, antique, and creamy—punctuated with small wooden or brown baskets parading across a salvaged fireplace mantel that acts as a headboard.

"Buy what you like, then mix and match. Everything doesn't have to go together perfectly." Judy of Manchester, Vermont

Dark and Handsome Check out the masculine side of the flea market spectrum. This bedroom is home to collections of bottles, signs, and old farm tools anchored by a vintage bed and a colorful handmade quilt. ❏

bathrooms

More than just a place to brush and floss in the morning, the bathroom needs a little tender loving care to maximize its potential. See how these clever baths make use of flea market treasures to glean extra storage and display space while gaining a little character in the process.

25

The Well-Furnished Bath Rather than commissioning an expensive custom vanity, keep your eyes peeled for a dresser or chest that you can outfit with a faucet, sink, and plumbing. The wide ledges on this handsome English vanity hold bath necessities as well as a vintage French shaving mirror.

26

Store More Instead of protecting pastries from pesky insects, an old Texas pie safe now holds fresh towels. The vanity is a prime example of mixing old and new items. Contemporary cabinets house a 19th-century high-collar porcelain sink that slips into a compatible stone countertop.

27

Put a Lid on It A group of crockery lids (often a bargain if chipped or cracked) echoes the curves of a contemporary sink. This grouping works because the lids are all white and of a similar size. Below them, a stack of old suitcases and baskets (widely available at flea markets) hides extra towels, toilet tissue, and other bathroom supplies.

28

29

30. Nice Legs You know what they say about another man's trash. This vanity features three of the original 12 balustrades salvaged from a curbside trash pile. (One is hidden by the fabric skirt.) A new vanity top and apron, both made of pine, are painted and sanded to match the old legs.

31. Completely Country Only in today's thoroughly country style bathroom could a flea market pitcher and washbasin sit so proudly next to a new pedestal sink. Other bargains, including an old stocking and hand towels, give this bath character. ❏

30

28. Have a Seat An office chair moonlights as a vanity seat and adjusts to the ideal height for applying makeup. Behind it, a 1920s medicine cabinet displays antique liquid measuring jars from a French apothecary. Their job is to keep cosmetics brushes organized and ready for use.

29. Bring the Outside In Outdoor elements are often perfectly at home inside, as this vanity area shows. The dressing table seems casual when partnered with a rusty French garden chair and green metal birdcage.

31

outdoor rooms
and gardens

Your home—and perhaps your attitude—can benefit from a little fresh air. Use your favorite flea market finds to blur the lines between indoors and out. Metal garden furniture thrives on a porch; old windows look even more appealing in a garden. So slow down, unwind, and enjoy the sunshine.

32

Charming Chairs Sturdy, old-fashioned café chairs need only a fresh coat of paint and simple seat cushions to take their place on a patio or deck. A 1950s tablecloth makes the matching metal table look almost regal.

33

More than a Door Look beyond an item's intended use. Here, a salvaged door blossoms into a potting bench with the addition of an old picket fence and shelves made of recycled wood.

34

Blooms with a View Cottage gardens, with their informal plantings, are perfect for showcasing salvaged pieces. Tucked behind a café table and chairs, this large window becomes an outdoor "wall" that gives the illusion of privacy. It also brings a linear element to an organic landscape.

36

37

35. Fresh Air Though enclosed, this room exhibits the ambience of an open porch or patio, thanks to outdoor elements like an old shutter, a birdhouse, and Adirondack-style furniture. A large cupboard sporting distressed blue paint anchors the room and provides a focal point.

36. So Very Aviary Painted birdhouses—long retired from sheltering our feathered friends—add line and texture to this sunroom. The cages' mellow hues and unusual shapes give them an architectural presence that complements the pottery and plants. Even better, they're inexpensive at flea markets and antiques shops.

37. New Use for an Old Bike A bicycle that has logged too many miles or has rusted beyond working order can be charming on a front stoop. For $5, plus the cost of an old locker-room basket (also a bargain), this bicycle can retire with dignity.

> "I like to display old lanterns and camping stuff from the 1950s and 1960s. It brings back childhood memories."
>
> Walter of Winchendon, Massachusetts

38. From the Garage to the Garden Trugs—which usually tote hammers, nails, and screws—can be purchased at junk shops for a mere $30 but are worth so much more for their get-organized capability. Use them in the garden to store pots, hand tools, or small flats of seedlings.

39. Party Pleaser The furniture selection in this sunroom says the space is made for entertaining. In addition to a comfy, casual sofa and chair, a tea cart stands in as a coffee table and can be used to serve drinks and snacks to party guests. ❏

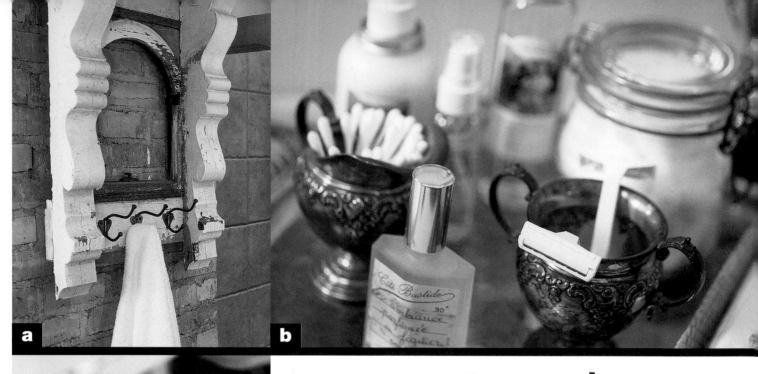

40 store it

a By adding metal hooks and hanging it outside the bathroom shower, this piece of architectural salvage is transformed into an ornate towel holder. **b** Small trophies—available in all shapes and sizes—hold cotton swabs and razors in this bath, adding a graceful presence when placed on a vanity tray with other interesting urns and containers. **c** Stacked document boxes (once part of an office setting) stash out-of-season clothing or extra blankets and bed linens. They also make an interesting "destination" at the end of this hallway and elevate an Alexander Calder stabile. **d** An antique wooden trough, old but still sturdy, can help with entertaining. Buy one that fits on your dining-room buffet or sideboard, and fill it with bowls of snacks and decorative plantings. You can easily move the trough from room to room for grazing guests, and then tote it back to the kitchen for refills. **e** Even though the milkman no longer delivers to your doorstep, this bottle

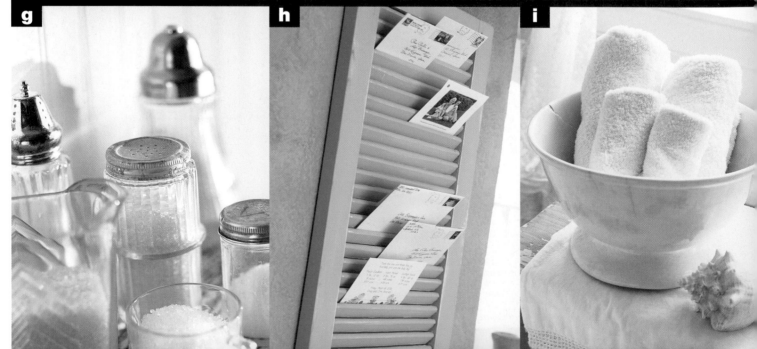

carrier can be put to good use as a kitchen-towel holder. **f** Vintage sacks, which once held feed, oats, or flour, make sturdy laundry bags. Hang a few on hooks in the laundry room to simplify the task of separating whites from colors and delicates. **g** Salt-and-pepper shakers are easy to find at flea markets, junk shops, and garage sales. These glass ones now hold bath salts and look charming when displayed near the tub. **h** Window shutters in all shapes, sizes, and colors dot flea markets. Hang a short one on the wall for organizing bills and other mail, or purchase a wider one for holding magazines and catalogs. **i** A chipped earthenware bowl may not be suitable for cooking duty in the kitchen but makes a homey addition to the bath—especially for the small (but important) task of holding hand towels. **j** Save egg cartons for storing delicate holiday ornaments. They stack neatly in a trunk or closet and can hold dozens of fragile items. **k** Scrolled metal brackets support a marble kitchen shelf that keeps bowls off the countertop when not in use. ❑

fabric fix-ups

Vintage fabrics—from ticking and feed sacks to quilts and tablecloths—are available by the bundle at flea markets. And depending on how much you grab, you can transform your woven treasure—large or small—into something that's both useful and beautiful.

Grandma's Idea Striped ticking was once the fabric of choice for encasing feather pillows. We like the fact that it's not hidden by pillowcases anymore. Make your own old-fashioned pillowcases by stitching the fabric to fit the desired forms, and then sewing buttons or hook-and-loop tape to the backs for closure. Pile the pillows in heaps on your porch furniture, and you're ready to relax.

41

43

42. Hang Up Your Apron June Cleaver never would have imagined that folks today would use aprons as wall decorations. Their vibrant patterns and charming details, such as rickrack and intricate stitching, are hard to resist—especially in a kitchen or breakfast room that celebrates 1950s style. This room's retro dinette set and punchy colored pottery are all flea market finds.

43. Slipcover in a Snap Who can argue with instant style? This textured slipcover was created by securing a chenille curtain panel to a sofa with safety pins. Not only does it give the room a casual attitude, the chenille is a cinch to clean—just throw it in the washer.

44. Put to Good Use Finding quilts in perfect condition is tough, even if you are willing to pay top dollar. Instead, look for easy-to-find stained or worn quilts that match your decor. You're sure to find pristine patches that are large enough to cover an ottoman, so you can park your feet in style.

45. Magic Sheets Because sheets are wider and cheaper than decorator fabric, they make excellent curtains for large windows. Use two twin flat sheets (or split a larger one and hem the raw edges), and sew a contrasting border to each edge. Stitch ribbon or fabric strips to the top edges, and then tie it to a curtain rod.

46

Lovable Misfits Flea market fabrics don't have to match perfectly—that's the secret of their charm. This overstuffed chair is designed for lounging— and it gets even comfier when you add pillows crafted from mismatched scraps of fabric and ribbon. Sheer curtains and off-white fabric add shimmer to the window and the lamp shade.

49. The Charm of Chenille Sink into softness. Textured, colorful chenille bedspreads are back. Find an unblemished one (you might discover one for as little as $30) to cover your bed, and save the stained or torn pieces for making coordinating pillow shams.

50. Bed-Blanket Bingo Don't hide those collectible blankets in the linen closet where no one can enjoy them. Instead, go vertical. Drape blankets with similar hues over your headboard to create a colorful padded surface. ❑

47. Hanging Out by the Fire Crackling flames point the way to striped wool blankets that hang above this oversized fireplace. A well-used rocking chair holds a ticking-covered pillow and a cozy throw, anticipating the next cup of tea.

48. Clean and Simple Turning old dish towels into café curtains is a snap. Simply cut them to the desired proportions, leaving room for the hems. After hemming the edges, decorate the towels with ribbon or rickrack, clip curtain rings to the top edges, and slide the rings onto a curtain rod.

furniture face-lifts

Dressers, beds, drawers, windows, and more … furniture and accessories in all sizes, shapes, and conditions beg for new owners at flea markets. As a savvy shopper, you can save money by buying imperfect pieces and refurbishing them in a way that suits your style. All it takes is a little money, some elbow grease, and a lot of imagination.

51

Bowling Anyone? This whimsical end table was created by attaching four bowling pins to a metal World War II case (originally used for gas masks) with drywall screws. The table, which now stores old photos, showcases classic gum-ball machines that work.

52

Sew Useful Painted and crowned with a new marble top, this old Singer sewing-machine base makes a convenient desk for writing letters or opening mail.

53

Born in a Barn A genuine barn-stall door was found at an auction, power-washed, and installed on a galvanized-steel sliding track. Now it can be closed to separate the family room from the stairway and porch.

54

56

55

57

54. Feetfirst Salvaged from a timeworn dresser, this old drawer becomes an ottoman with the addition of four legs (purchased at a home center), white paint, and an upholstered top. A hinged top allows the piece to double as a small storage chest.

55. Stack 'em Up A collection of orphaned drawers now stores odds and ends, thanks to a saw and a screwdriver. The drawers are housed in ¾-inch plywood boxes that are screwed together. The whole piece is mounted on casters for mobility.

56. Fine Furniture Originally a sideboard found at an auction, this piece now functions as a double vanity in a master bathroom. Most dressers and sideboards can be converted into vanities by cutting holes in the top for the sink and in the back for the plumbing.

57. Giddyap! What better way to set off a cowboy-themed chenille bedspread and Beacon blankets than with hot-off-the-trail accessories? Use wagon wheels for twin-size headboards and a window—they'll finish off a western-style room that any budding cowboy or cowgirl would love.

58

From Window to Cupboard If a worn, cast-off window catches your eye, consider giving it a second chance at life. By constructing a three-sided box to fit the window and then installing the window to the front with flat hinges, you can create a primitive-style cupboard that's perfect for displaying pottery and other treasures.

59 **Approach the Bench** An antique English walnut bed in poor condition (purchased for $100) becomes an impressive bench on a covered porch. The secret is shortening the side rails to make a comfortable seating depth and then securing the rails with L-shape brackets and screws. Support the upholstered cushion with an additional 1×4 board, and you can kick back and relax.

"Furniture is not a bargain if it doesn't fit. Measure your space before you shop, and check the piece with a tape measure before you buy."

Kathie of Camden, Maine

Makeover Magic Once free for the taking, this rickety dresser is now a stylish conversation piece. Between the rescue and its current use for display, the dresser's sides, top, bottom, and drawer pieces were stripped and cut to the desired depth. Shelves were cut for the lower drawer spaces and attached with dowels. Painted flowers and a coat of stain give the piece room-ready presence. ❏

metal makeovers

From lacy garden gates to discarded baking pans and industrial salvage,

cast-off metal offers a wealth of options for making personal style statements.

A little creative thinking goes a long way toward finding unique uses for

all things metal.

61

In the Bedroom Feel free to bring the outdoors in. Here, a garden-gate pediment was welded to two wrought-iron fence posts to create a dramatic headboard. It looks regal behind a bed piled with plump, multicolored pillows.

62

Hardware as Art A tie bolt from a church in Brooklyn looks like a modern sculpture when showcased on this dining room wall. Iron brackets from an old fence support the kitchen mantel, which displays a massive wooden mold for making steel cogs.

63

From Dairy to Dessert Dairy farmers once sat on this kind of stool to milk their cows. Cleaned and brought into the house, it makes an ideal cake stand.

64. Bucket Brigade New Englanders used to collect tree sap in buckets like these. Now the colorful containers serve as artwork. Additional metal accents include a rusted wastebasket, an old wire basket, and a candleholder; they take on almost sculptural qualities when placed just so on a coffee table.

65. Storage Pan Cast-iron muffin and bread pans are easy as pie to find at flea markets, and they're often reasonably priced. These pans become office-supply catchalls when placed on a desk. Also try them in the kitchen for appetizers or condiments.

66. Tin Is In Tin ceiling tiles—once a hallmark of elaborate Victorian homes—make unique and interesting wall art. Use molding or scrap lumber to frame a single tile, conceal any sharp edges, and make the tile look like artwork. ❑

a

b

67 display it

a Purchase prints that are similar in size and color; don't worry about unmatched frames or orientation. Arrange them over a headboard for a striking bedroom focal point. **b** Show off a hard-won dishware collection by lining shelves with lace, allowing the scallops to peek over the edges. **c** Different items can work together on the same mantel—just mix the scales and textures. Here, a mirror with a white chipped-paint frame is the largest element, balanced by a wall-hung plate and a pair of tea lamps flanking a gold-framed print. A glazed statue completes the arrangement. **d** Even if you didn't win them, old trophies are still prized finds. Group several to make the most of their curvaceous shapes. **e** Instead of using them, stack linens on a table. Or hang a treasured garment on the wall to lend any room a homespun feel. **f** Wooden benches are inexpensive; scoop up more than one for displaying plants or baskets. **g** The key to showing off pottery is in the arrangement. Here, pottery in

f

h

i

various shapes, sizes, and colors (though all in blues or greens) light up glass shelves. If possible, display items on recessed shelves to keep them out of harm's way. Experiment with the placement of each piece until you find a pleasing configuration. **h** This vignette, which displays a group of lamps, is another example of showcasing flea market finds. (Rule of thumb: Three or more of anything qualifies as a collection.) Interesting backdrops, such as this chipped-paint door and table, add visual texture. **i** Shell-encrusted items are definitely see-worthy—they're one of today's hottest collecting trends. This grouping is symmetrical and is anchored by two tall statues; smaller pieces are elevated so they don't get lost in the shuffle. **j** Attached to clips and threaded onto a chain strung above a doorway, old family photos are brought out of the attic and given the attention they deserve. **k** Show off your green thumb—and multiple colors of pottery—by arranging potted plants on a ladder. **l** For a glorious seasonal display, a tall trough filled with gourds, squash, and pumpkins can't be beat. Change the arrangement to suit the season. ❑

always changing

Dallas interiors-shop owner Kelly O'Neal says he doesn't mind doing a little work around the house. But in his case, "a little" is an understatement. He is constantly making minor adjustments to update his already stylish, urban-flavored digs. His secret for staying on budget? Scouring flea markets for one-of-a-kind treasures.

68

International Flavor Exotic yet functional, this coffee table was originally a window shutter in India. Several of the exotic items in Kelly's den were purchased on international buying trips.

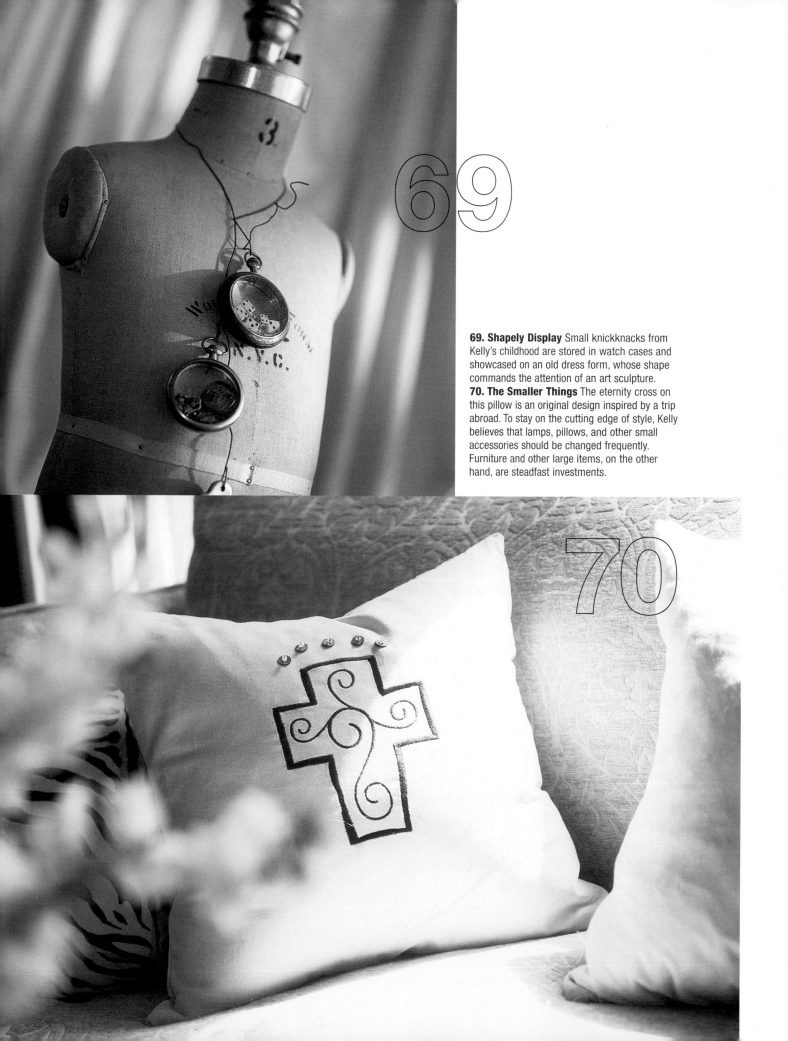

69

69. Shapely Display Small knickknacks from Kelly's childhood are stored in watch cases and showcased on an old dress form, whose shape commands the attention of an art sculpture.

70. The Smaller Things The eternity cross on this pillow is an original design inspired by a trip abroad. To stay on the cutting edge of style, Kelly believes that lamps, pillows, and other small accessories should be changed frequently. Furniture and other large items, on the other hand, are steadfast investments.

70

71. Fridge Face-Lift Bored with his old refrigerator but not willing to spend $2,000 on a new one, Kelly got creative: He decoupaged book pages to the sides of his existing fridge. Decoupaging is a decorative technique that involves applying paper cutouts to a surface and sealing them with glue. It can brilliantly transform an old, tired piece into something fresh.

72. Bargain Room The dining room cupboard was an auction bargain, and the table belonged to a friend who considered it trash. "Unless I really, really love it, I won't pay top dollar for anything," Kelly says. His favorite item in the house is the wall hanging, which is from a church in North Carolina.

"Unless I really, really love it," Kelly declares, "I won't pay top dollar for anything."

Best of Both Worlds The master bedroom is a prime example of mixing the old with the new. Kelly designed the bed and covered it with new linens in classic patterns. An old secretary that he purchased from a church in Ecuador adds the final touch.

74

Show-Off A French pot rack holds fresh towels and displays other items without taking up precious floor space. Kelly stripped the existing window frame, intending to repaint it, but decided he liked the distressed look and left it as is. ❏

fresh and feminine

Decorator and antiques dealer Amy Krogh specializes in cottage style at home and at work. Lively patterned fabric, jubilant paint colors, and furniture made for lounging are the hallmarks of cottage decorating. Amy's advice on colors, collections, and comfy room settings will help you bring country's most popular look home.

75. Color Connection Amy uses color to pull together mixed groupings, such as these Homer Laughlin Orange Tree bowls interspersed with 1940s vases and pitchers.

76. Sweet Slipcovers These slipcovers, which are sewn from vintage bark cloth combined with new white and blue fabrics, are beautiful and durable. Cream moldings and pine furnishings prevent the room from overdosing on pastels.

76

77. Put to Good Use A salvaged mantel proudly holds old watering cans aloft for an outdoor, flea market feel in the living room. Chipped and weathered paint on the coffee table, mantel, and stool testify to Amy's desire that her house be comfortable. "Everything in a room should be meant to be touched," she says. "I only buy things with the intent to use them."
78. Sweep of Softness Vintage, lace-edged linens are layered on the hutch's door, which is kept open to show off the items inside. "I really think textiles are a huge part of making a room look comfortable," Amy says.

79. Clever Curtains When Amy found a vintage tablecloth in the right colors for her kitchen, she wasn't deterred by the holes in its center. She merely clipped off the pristine corners and turned them into cheery valances. Additional examples of vintage pottery in fresh yellows and soft teals dot the room.

80. Sun-Washed Color A well-worn, freshly painted side table topped with vintage fabric, a periwinkle bowl, and coffee and tea containers—all flea market finds—flavor the kitchen with the essence of cottage. The weathered colors glow against the yellow walls. "For me, yellow is a no-fall wall color," Amy says. "It works great with everything, especially soft, faded reds and blues."

81

81. Better than New Softer colors rule the upstairs, which is evident in this paneled bathroom that combines delicious periwinkle with crisp white. Amy replaced the standard bathroom cabinet and lighting with antique pieces.

82. A Mixed Bouquet Combining several florals in the master bedroom is a refreshing change of pace. The patterns "are completely different flowers and really vary in scale, but they work together because they have the same hues," Amy says. ❏

country pioneers

The cutting edge of country decorating is steeped in salvaged items, flea market bargains, and trash turned into treasures. It's flavored with a dollop of heritage and a healthy dash of free spirit, as shown in Fred and Wendy Testu's San Francisco townhouse.

83

Cultural Fusion An unusual mix of drill bits and old photographs enlivens a Mission-style tabletop. The wax crown is a traditional bridal headdress in the French region where Fred grew up.

84

A Time for Every Purpose Time stands still in this bedroom, where a rustic clock that once graced a French church now hangs. A trunk and a suitcase at the foot of the bed bring the warmth of wood and leather and provide convenient places for storage.

Rusty, Not Rustic An antique baby bed, softened with cushions covered in toile and ticking, makes a suitable companion for an old-fashioned tricycle—both flea market bargains. Above the slipcovered table, a parade of old medicine bottles displays Wendy's handmade porcelain tulips.

A Natural Environment Mixing metal furnishings with plants and other natural objects is one of Fred and Wendy's favorite ways to decorate. In their living room, the thin lines of gently aged café chairs and a daybed quietly echo the slender, sculptural birch branches.

87. Organic Experience Fusing disparate pieces into eye-catching room settings is a Testu trademark. Here, weathered porch furniture plumped with awning-stripe cushions echoes the lines in the salvaged ironwork on the wall. Plants also play a large role in this room. Upside-down goblets hold forced bulbs, and grass grows in a bidet-turned-planter.

88. Natural Way A mellow length of wood with a hole for the sink disguises a standard countertop. Enamel canisters pay tribute to Fred's French heritage.

89. A Coat of Wood Wary of anything artificial or high-tech, Fred found the look of their refrigerator so offensive that he wrapped it in old barn wood as a surprise for Wendy. ❏

87

88

"Many things we like are rough," Fred says. "We use a lot of metal."
"We are into rust, not rustic," Wendy jokes.

89

colonial times

A vintage Connecticut farmhouse proved to be perfect for John and Christiane Oliviera Weiss's eclectic decorating tastes. He favors lots of stuff, while she prefers a clean-line style. Filled with piles of collectibles and a colorful mix of furnishings, their home possesses one-of-a-kind character.

90

Casual Mix Just inside the front door, the living room sets the decorating tone for the house by blending old (a vintage trunk turned into a coffee table and bench) with new (the sofa, chair, rug, and accessories).

First Impression John and Christiane's entryway is awash in their collections and includes stacks of round boxes, wooden crates, and other items they've acquired over the years. "I never stick with any one period," says John. "Everything is fair game."

91

92. Neutral Territory Simple white woodwork, fireplace bricks, a distressed wood floor, and soft-colored walls provide a neutral backdrop to the carefully collected artifacts found in the living room.

93. Focal Point Lounging on the sofa is the perfect way to admire an early-period painting and an intricate wrought-iron candleholder (both signature Colonial elements). The mantel clock makes its own classic statement.

94. Thinking of Yesterday Another decorating classic, "The Thinker," is used in duplicate as bookends that steady a few old tomes. Tall, distressed candlesticks throw the coffee table a few curves.

95. Bottoms Up The red bar in the dining room displays old seltzer bottles, whiskey bottles, and cocktail shakers. The bar's ruddy lines draw attention to the still-life above, which was purchased at a tag sale for $2.

96. Dark and Rich The 1930s desk is the centerpiece of the downstairs family room, where the Weisses' style takes charge. Collectibles of all sorts—globes, lighters, movie projectors, cameras, books—pack the built-in shelving and line the walls. "It's my favorite and most-used room," John says.

97. Alfresco Dining New ladder-back chairs surround an old country style trestle table in the window-lined dining room. An antique corner cabinet displays a pottery collection, and benches around the room can be pulled up to the table for extra seating. Primitive style furniture is perfect for the casual atmosphere the couple enjoys.

"If an object turns out to be highly sought after or valuable, that's a bonus," John says, "but not why I bought it."

96

98. Be Our Guest The guest room is constantly in use by John and Christiane's friends and family. Flea market items, such as the bedside table, lamp, and throw pillow, make the space feel cozy and familiar.

99. Tag-Sale Tableau A gleaming Victorian desk (found at a tag sale) displays old family photos and letters, antique bottles, and a vintage typewriter, creating a lovely vignette that's sure to enthrall the Weisses' guests.

Instant Age Character-laden antiques—such as the trunk, armoire, side table, and leather suitcases—warm the relatively new master bedroom. This room was added to the house by the previous owners and features a simple wall color and unpretentious linens, which appeal to Christiane's clean, fresh decorating style. ❏

Garden
STYLE

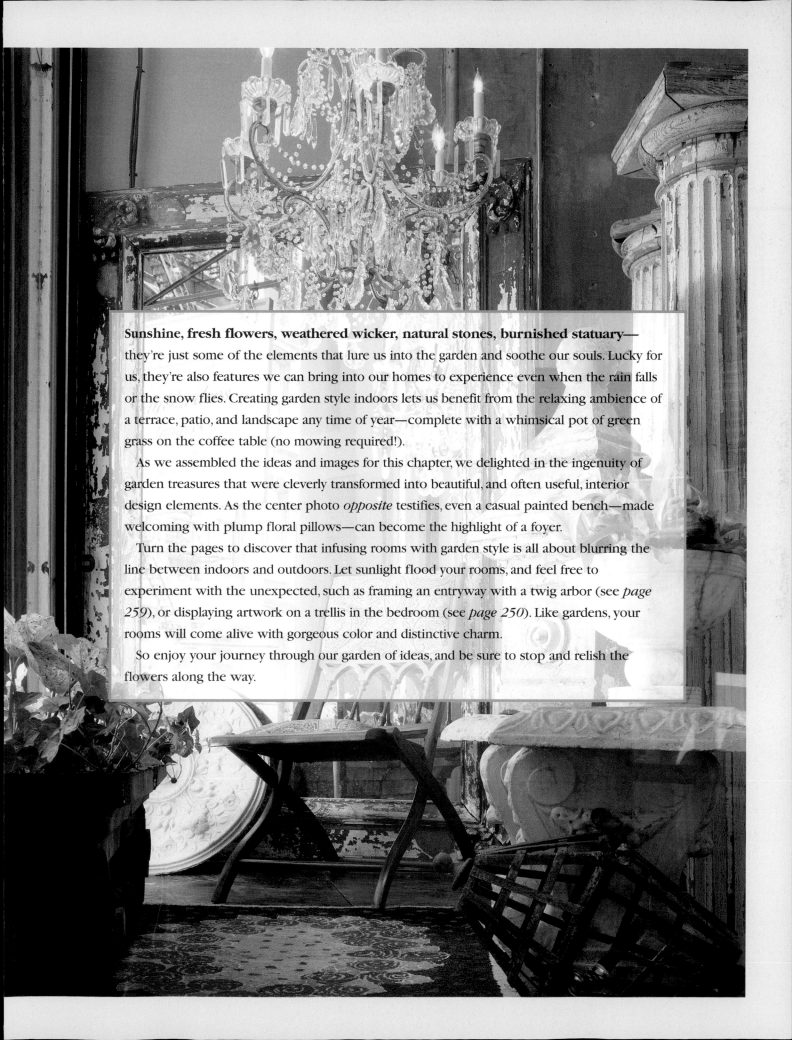

Sunshine, fresh flowers, weathered wicker, natural stones, burnished statuary— they're just some of the elements that lure us into the garden and soothe our souls. Lucky for us, they're also features we can bring into our homes to experience even when the rain falls or the snow flies. Creating garden style indoors lets us benefit from the relaxing ambience of a terrace, patio, and landscape any time of year—complete with a whimsical pot of green grass on the coffee table (no mowing required!).

As we assembled the ideas and images for this chapter, we delighted in the ingenuity of garden treasures that were cleverly transformed into beautiful, and often useful, interior design elements. As the center photo *opposite* testifies, even a casual painted bench—made welcoming with plump floral pillows—can become the highlight of a foyer.

Turn the pages to discover that infusing rooms with garden style is all about blurring the line between indoors and outdoors. Let sunlight flood your rooms, and feel free to experiment with the unexpected, such as framing an entryway with a twig arbor (see *page 259*), or displaying artwork on a trellis in the bedroom (see *page 250*). Like gardens, your rooms will come alive with gorgeous color and distinctive charm.

So enjoy your journey through our garden of ideas, and be sure to stop and relish the flowers along the way.

*garden*style

when it comes to creating a garden style interior, you'll find that details energize your efforts. Whether you harvest accessories, tools, and architectural fragments from the garden or patio, or tote home flea market treasures that feature gardenlike motifs, they're all ideal for infusing rooms with style inspired by the outdoors. These small yet mighty features provide dazzle that's easy to change on a whim. Move any of these garden accents from room to room, or tuck them away and substitute something new to suit the season. The possibilities for creating different looks are as unlimited as nature's creations.

accent on **entertaining**

1

Treat your guests to a one-of-a-kind tabletop display when you entertain. On this round, skirted dining table, favorite plants are mixed with ornamental finials and pottery. Long-lasting orchids in antique-finish pots enliven the thoughtful arrangement of fruit and foliage.

combine old and new

A vintage wire plant stand, a charming farm table and bench, and a trio of distressed shelves set the stage to show off a wide assortment of garden accents. Cut flowers and blooming plants lend color to this magical mix.

hunt for **bargains**

Scour flea markets and yard sales for bargain garden style collections to display indoors or outdoors, such as these folk art birdhouses, the rustic feeder, and the old-fashioned watering can.

enchant with ivory

4

Decorated with ivory creamware, pottery, and porcelains, this stylishly eclectic dining room reflects the mood of an all-white garden. Because they are monochromatic, the disparate objects and shapes work well together. Botanical prints in ivory frames introduce understated color.

contrast creates drama

Throw a few surprises into your one-color scheme. To create a dramatic
contrast, this dark-wood Victorian-era cabinet and black tray table offer a
refreshing juxtaposition to the all-white collection on the adjacent wall.

design with romance at **heart**

6

Surrounded by a beautiful blend of vintage and reproduction accents, this sofa—with its gently curved arms and ruffled skirt—lends romance to the living area. Flower-motif pillows provide a soft garden style link to the trellis candle stand, woven basket, and unusual architectural fragments.

stack up for style

A woven picnic basket, well-used tables, and primitive
wooden boxes create a striking stair-step display for a mix
of fragments, finials, and found accents. On the wall, an
intricate section of ironwork serves as art.

study the shapes

8

Displayed on rustic wooden shelves suspended from an old door, this all-white collection of reproduction urns, a finial, and a birdhouse becomes a study in shapes and shadows.

enjoy everyday objects

9

Everyday objects can evolve into elements of style and beauty, such as this pair of bottles arranged beneath an aged table, where they double as vases for dried allium. Two woven picnic baskets are stacked beside the bottles for visual balance.

bring country to the **suburbs**

10

A suburban deck gains instant "age" when trimmed with a salvaged railing fragment. The original red paint pairs with a shallow bowl of blooms, bringing bursts of color to the weathered-wood deck and bench.

style with fragments and **finds**

11

Once you discover an object you love at a flea market or other venue, don't pass it up just because you're not sure what to do with it—you may never find another just like it. Unusual treasures, such as this shapely wooden baluster and leafy lamp base, for example, can be grouped to form a striking tabletop display.

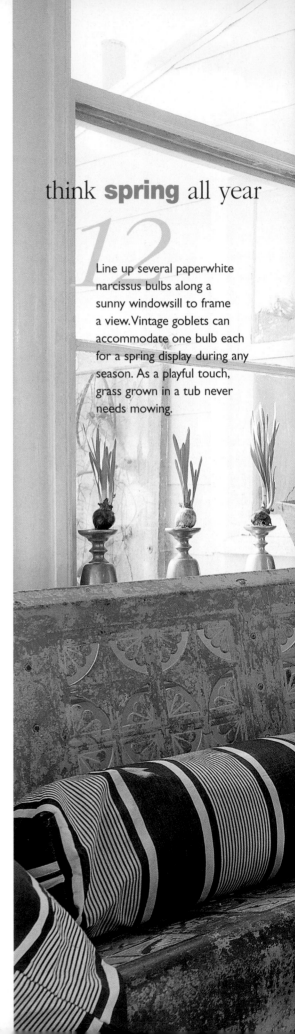

think **spring** all year

12

Line up several paperwhite narcissus bulbs along a sunny windowsill to frame a view. Vintage goblets can accommodate one bulb each for a spring display during any season. As a playful touch, grass grown in a tub never needs mowing.

create alfresco dining **indoors**

13

Bistro chairs, charmingly dressed in an assortment of original colors, work well for creating an outdoor dining atmosphere indoors. A child's vintage wheelbarrow is an unexpected flower-filled centerpiece on the table.

experiment with ordinary objects

14

Use ordinary garden items in uncommon ways. This pale pink bistro chair doubles as a pretty place to display potted and cut flowers. Teamed with architectural fragments, it transforms an empty spot on the terrace into a focal point.

spice up your **spaces**

15

Watch for unusual accents to transform plain walls and furnishings into distinctive decorative assets. This nondescript white chest of drawers gained charming character by trading plain knobs for playful garden-theme pulls. Three-dimensional plaques lend a fanciful look to the walls as well. ❏

front porches invite neighbors to walk up and chat. Side porches encourage reading, talking, and relaxing. Back porches bring the garden indoors. Whatever your house and setting, there are few things more fun than a swing, a glass of lemonade, and a long, lazy afternoon on the porch. Porches are in vogue for both remodeling and new construction, as families look for ways to create casual fresh-air rooms and retreats. If you have one, enrich your haven with comfortable furnishings, a ceiling fan, and plants. If you don't, a porch addition may be the remodeling project you need to bring garden style into your home.

porch *pleasures*

pair a **swing** with rockers

16

Take advantage of your porch by starting with the basics—a porch swing and sturdy rockers with woven seats. Add familiar living room elements, such as braided rag rugs and tables for drinks and flowers.

energize with a patterned rug

For fun, mix a colorful, durable kilim or dhurrie rug with oversize twig and smaller-scale dining furniture. Introduce favorite outdoor touches, such as the substantial corbel and wire plant stand, to create your version of lighthearted garden style.

enliven with blue and white

18

Think classic color combinations, such as blue and white, for porch furniture. As you search for the right furnishings, include versatile wicker trunks as display and serving pieces that also offer storage for cushions, table linens, and other items.

collect comfortable **furnishings**

19

Vintage and reproduction furniture and accessories easily mix to transform this bayside screened porch into an inviting living and dining room. The secret to unifying disparate pieces? White paint and blue-and-white stripes.

capture cooling **breezes**

20

Porches are perfect for capturing cooling breezes and bringing them into the house. Here, pairs of French doors open the interior spaces to this shady retreat.

Pairs of French doors blur the line between indoors and outdoors, allowing you to expand entertaining space.

paint **flowers** overhead

21

Take advantage of the charm of a beaded-board ceiling with an overhead garden of painted blossoms and colorful leaves. Choose a pretty color, such as this yellow, or the traditional pale green or blue used for porch ceilings.

play up the **architecture**

22

Dress up your porch to make a positive first impression with passersby and visitors. Hefty turned posts and decorative spindles give this porch character, and the round opening makes it intriguing.

create a spot to **sleep**

23

Screening in a porch makes it more usable, allowing the space to perform as a living area or as a breezy spot for snoozing. This sunny sleeping porch was created as a fun place for the grandchildren to bunk overnight.

enjoy your **vintage** wicker

24

For porch furniture that never looks dated, shop for restored and reproduction white wicker in comfortable shapes and sizes. A mix of fabric patterns, plants, and accessories makes it easy to change the look with the season or the special occasion. ❏

living spaces

when you love garden style, you can live with a relaxed look that's fun to change with your current interests and newest finds. Do you like old iron gates, picket fences, and garden benches? Do you appreciate rooms that open wide with sleek garden furniture and oversized planters? Do you love the charm of distressed furniture and vintage botanical prints? With carefully chosen elements, your garden style can translate into your decorating style. If the style is new to you, start where you feel most comfortable. Accessories, such as small urns or garden-motif pottery, are ideal items to collect without making a major investment.

decorate two **spaces** as one

25

Unify your porch and living room by painting indoor and outdoor furniture in crisp, summery white. Mismatched wood pieces, such as this small desk and chair, enjoy renewed style, courtesy of fresh paint and snappy fabric.

add **roses** to a painted trellis

26

Paint walls a cheerful yellow, and detail below the chair rail with a freehand-painted French blue trellis and stylized flowers. To contrast with the bold wall, simplify furnishings by using white wicker for seating and blue-and-white plates for art.

relax with an age-worn **bench**

27

Re-create the refined ambience of a formal garden in your foyer with a gently distressed English-style outdoor bench. The delicate shape pairs nicely with dark woods and traditional furniture. A basket of freshly cut flowers relaxes the scene.

dial up **art**

28

Originally used by French astronomers, handsome iron sundials have long graced formal European and American gardens. Bring one inside as a focal point in a serene living room of soft neutral colors, pottery, and seasonal flowers.

start with a **colorful** floral

29

If you enjoy bright colors, look for floral fabrics in your favorite shades. Here, a cotton print sets a clear-red-and-pale-green scheme that is enhanced by distressed-wood shelves and a reclaimed desk and office chair.

bring **outdoor** furniture inside

30

Adirondack chairs brought in from the garden revitalize this quaint cottage style living room. Green paint ties the formerly white brick fireplace to the new garden look, and a section of picket fence creates a charming focal point above the mantel.

plant a garden urn

31

One great piece can make a garden style room. Look for a large outdoor urn, pot, or planter for seasonal flowers or plants. An overscaled basket for books or magazines is the perfect accent for this comfortable reading nook.

re-create **resort** chic

32

Contemporary style warms up to the outdoors when you start with the sleek, overscaled pieces that are typically associated with Southern California homes and gardens. Here, a woven storage ottoman doubles as a table.

hang **drapes** on branches

33

Decorate your living room in French garden style with a mix of the rustic and the refined. Here, a wrought iron daybed sets a fanciful mood that's reinforced by a skirted table and draperies that hang from twig branches. Leaf-trimmed lamp shades provide playful accents.

paint a park bench

34

What could be a friendlier way to welcome guests to your home
than a bench, painted classic green, in your entry hall? Plump floral pillows
and a woven cotton rag rug contribute comfort and fresh color.

accent red with **prints**

35

Enthusiasts of deep hues choose dark walls as a dramatic backdrop for floral prints, painted porcelains, and majolica-style pottery pieces. Pale tea-dyed fabrics and quilts translate cottage charm to a city setting. ❑

display on a **baker's** rack

36

Design a dining room in a snap by using
a baker's rack for plants and collectibles.
Mix a rugged reproduction pine table
with a garden bench, fruit-motif pillows,
and metal outdoor chairs, and create a
fanciful grouping that comes to life.

timeless dining

garden style offers tasteful, timeless elements that work equally well in the dining room and on the terrace. Here, yellow-and-white stripes on the walls establish a cabanalike atmosphere for meals. Black wrought iron shelves are a striking counterpoint to sunny yellow linens and fruit motifs while providing welcome display space for the room. The natural wood tones of the pine table and mahogany chairs lend warmth to the setting. A ficus tree in the sunlit alcove and bouquets of cut flowers on the table and shelves enliven the space with garden color.

update with lime green

37

Indoors and out, you can dress up a dining table with classic black-and-white toile, the French-style print that features pastoral outdoor scenes. Wherever you dine, brighten the mood with an overskirt and casual check napkins. In this case, lime green provides visual pizzazz.

reflect the **outdoors**

38

Multiply the light in a sunny dining setting by hanging a large mirror on a wall opposite windows. This round wrought iron beauty mimics the sun to play up the room-brightening theme.

Garden style dining begins with ample sunlight. Unadorned windows direct the eye to the furnishings and flowers.

design with Mother Nature

39

Spiderweb-back dining chairs and a lacy open-weave tablecloth contribute to the spacious, sunlit appeal of this white dining room. Vases and carafes filled with fresh garden flowers dress the table in easy elegance.

freshen your finds with white

40

For summer year-round, paint your dining room walls and
furniture in soft shades of white, and add collections of
white planters and containers. Accessories, plants, plates,
and art stand out against such a clean backdrop.

borrow from **formal** gardens

41

When your dining goal is a dressy version of garden style, incorporate iron terrace chairs with tie-on cushions. The iron is repeated in the scrolled, marble-topped console and rods for the sheers. Ficus trees in Chinese-style pots flank the console for visual balance.

invite a flock of **birdhouses**

42

Group and display the fruits of your collecting passions. Decorative shelves and a country pine table hold a village of whimsical birdhouses. Worn shutters, hinged together, serve as a rustic corner screen.

dine with a garden view

43 Bring a bistro table indoors for the year-round ambience of garden dining. All you need is a small table to skirt and a pair of outdoor chairs. Hang a moss-lined container of ivy and flowers, and the mood is complete. ❑

freshen up *with*
flowers
and containers

treat yourself to rooms brightened with armloads of fresh flowers gathered from your own garden or purchased from local florists and farmer's markets. To display blossoms, stray from standard florist's vases and search for containers with character. Collectible pottery, vintage metal buckets, and cast-iron urns are just some of the options available at flea markets, auctions, and yard sales.

When you're ready to arrange a bouquet, position flowers or leaves to spill over the container rim. Insert flower faces to radiate outward from the center of the container, with some looking down, some out, and some up. Allow vines or long stems to gracefully tumble and cascade toward the tabletop, creating design interest and a feeling of motion.

go country with **crockery**

44

A stoneware crock is a good container for creating a lavish bouquet. Crumple chicken wire to fill the crock and hold stems in place. Remove the leaves along the lower three-fourths of the stems to prevent leaves from rotting in the water and to allow more stems in the arrangement.

beautify with dried flowers

45

Dried flowers offer lasting beauty with minimal upkeep. Rather than being placed in containers, these dried delphiniums, eucalyptus, calla lilies, baby's breath, and roses are suspended from the bedposts.

surprise with **fruit**

46

Frequent farmer's markets to find fruits to add as unexpected accents. These tiny unripened plums have an apricot blush that blends beautifully with the color of Old Timer hybrid tea roses.

multiply for **magic**

47

Instead of fashioning one big arrangement, make three small ones. The soft silver color of pewter sets off these vibrant reds. This grouping includes Russell lupines, anemones, scabiosa, chocolate cosmos, pansies, roses, and rose foliage.

fill up with **roses**

48

If you have a prolific rosebush, it's difficult to overdo the beauty of a rose-filled urn. To create a lush blooming look, start at the rim of the vase, and cut stems short enough to position flower faces at the rim or slightly lower. Cut the remaining stems about the same length, and insert them to create a mound.

keep the look **casual**

49

Blend old-time favorites—such as delphinium, sweet pea, columbine, yarrow, and cosmos—to create a beautiful bouquet. With such a majestic mix, you don't have to be an expert at arranging flowers. The slightly haphazard appearance only adds to the charm.

gather riches from the roadside

50

Some of the best things in life are free. For a burst of
color, combine summer perennials with roadside gleanings.
If your rustic container, such as this syrup bucket, isn't
watertight, insert a widemouthed jar to hold the bouquet.

51

Even when you have a specific color scheme, you can introduce new colors through flowers. In this fresh white, blue, and yellow living room, a simple bouquet of one type of flower in a pitcher injects a splash of color.

learn about urns

organize clutter

52

Even without flowers, special containers add beauty to practicality. Consider these options for using an urn. Here, it organizes by holding magazines and other items you want to keep.

display and cool **wine**

53

Fill an urn with ice, and chill your favorite wines and champagnes in casual garden style. Of course, this idea works just as well for sodas, lemonade, teas, and bottled water. Place the urn on the porch or patio for outdoor parties. Indoors, it's a portable bar, standing on a barrel or countertop with glasses nearby.

cast a pleasing **glow**

54

For a holiday focal point, place a large pillar candle in the center of an urn, and fill around it with mixed nuts in the shell. If the urn is quite deep, place a terra-cotta pot upside down inside it to raise the candle to the desired height. Fill in with crumpled newspapers to within an inch of the rim, and then add nuts. Finish with seasonal fruit and foliage arranged around the base.

create a bread**basket**

55

Crusty loaves of bread launch a build-your-own-sandwich buffet. Spread a tea towel over the mouth of the urn, and arrange the breads. Have a breadboard and knife nearby to cut slices. ❏

beautiful
bedrooms

sleep soundly surrounded by
serenity. Be generous with floral-motif fabrics,
and pair them with distressed woods, ornate
ironwork, and a profusion of garden-related
artwork, collections, and architectural salvage
pieces. Round out your tranquil retreat by
layering a bed with clouds of linens in
complementary patterns or in tones of
room-refreshing white and ivory.

romance with **florals**

Garner the warmth and romance of a summer garden for a guest bedroom using delicately sponged walls and a gently distressed table topped with white and silver accents. Here, pretty floral-print panels flank the table, imitating a window treatment, to soften the setting and enhance the subtle palette.

compose a **vignette**

57

A vintage linen tablecloth and a flea market table make an ideal foundation for composing a garden style vignette. Here, a porch-balustrade lamp and a pair of arched iron grates interplay with aged silver and a tall candle stand.

fashion furniture from **fragments**

58

Architectural fragments become stylish furnishings in this bedroom. The trunk, fashioned from pressed ceiling tins, teams with a coffee-table base made from an aged column capital and a bed constructed from salvaged columns and a decorative gable.

use **garden** gear in new ways

59

A salvaged trellis is a clever way to display art in this bedroom, and a wire plant stand holds plants and magazine-filled metal buckets. Hatboxes, old suitcases stacked as a table, and decorative corner shelves provide additional storage.

express floral endearment

60

Make any bed more inviting by plumping up the headboard with a profusion of pillows. In this pleasant bedroom, pillows and linens covered with vintage fabrics lend color and initiate the flower theme of the entire room. ❏

architectural salvage

though old houses may eventually expire after years of neglect, forward-thinking urban miners from around the country continue to rescue the elements that convey the spirit of the structure and capture our hearts. Shapely corbels, stately columns, intricate ironwork, and gracious garden ornaments are only a sampling of the treasures often salvaged from facades and landscapes. Worn surfaces and weathered finishes ignite the imagination, serving as reminders that these pieces have traveled through time.

Wordlessly, these treasures press us to determine their provenance, sparking lively debates that make them perfect for enlivening rooms with unforgettable garden style and vintage character. While architectural salvage yards abound throughout the country, you'll also discover these wonderful weathered elements at yard and estate sales, antiques stores, and flea markets. We found a variety of venues around the country that offer architectural and garden-related salvage in their merchandise mix. Their displays are inspirations, too. Enjoy the hunt.

try something **prominent**

61

As stand-alone focal points, stately elements such as these that have been salvaged from courtyards, formal gardens, and grand fences are hard to beat. Typically made of concrete or sturdy metals, these pieces are usually in good shape. Don't worry about minor damage—it only adds to the appeal.

create an elegant **ironwork** console

62

An intriguing section of iron balcony railing becomes
an elegant base for a console table when topped with glass.
Other salvaged ironwork pieces, such as a vent grate or garden
gate, could be adapted for the same purpose. Above the
table, a gracefully arched window casement serves
as a beguiling frame for a mirror.

mix touchable **textures**

63

Part of the pleasure of collecting architectural salvage is arranging the fascinating shapes and tantalizing textures. Here, your eye is easily drawn from the rusty lantern on the floor to the concrete bench, marble planter, and metal finial. The impressive pair of wooden columns calls attention to a tall ceiling. It's a smart way to turn an ordinary corner into a striking scene.

dress up the table

64

For dinner parties or as a daily display, architectural fragments and small garden urns become notable conversation pieces when arranged on a dining table.

combine eclectic **finishes**

65

Discover the wealth of handsome finishes created by decades spent outdoors. However you mix them, the finishes complement one another, as these weathered brass lanterns and black urn prove.

Time and Mother Nature work together to create beautifully rich patinas.

bring the outdoors in

66

Once exiled to the courtyard, these graceful concrete benches and their matching table make perfect dining companions when brought indoors. Paper lanterns and a weathered concrete planter contribute to the refreshing garden style setting.

install salvage **underfoot**

67

Slabs of natural stones, reclaimed from patio and porch floors, set the stage for garden style indoors. These hefty slate rectangles team with a border of small slate tiles to introduce an earth-friendly ambience in this casual dining area.

dramatically **define** an entry

68

A rustic arbor makes an unexpected and welcoming appearance on the interior of this entryway. Fashioned from branches, the arbor dramatically defines the doorway while framing the view beyond the handsome Gothic garden chairs.

hunt for beautiful **backdrops**

69

Lend depth and dimension to a windowless wall with a collection of exterior shutters still dressed in peeling paint. Here, a sunburst architectural piece is the center of attention, standing in as artwork refined by nature.

style with **statuary**

70

Garden statuary commands attention wherever you place it. This regal lion, for example, stands guard over a tabletop collection of topiaries.

71

Once you buy an intriguing salvage piece, you may find yourself hunting for companion pieces. These European pots are beautiful alone, but grouped as a collection, they make an even more memorable garden style statement.

Like snowflakes, no two salvaged pieces are alike. Time makes each one distinctive.

freshen up with **vintage** white

White refreshes almost any room, and you often can find salvaged garden and architectural pieces still wearing their original white paint. These intricate iron garden chairs, the stately pair of urns, and a vintage wooden potting table make this room bright and airy.

discover more than salvage

73

Keep your eyes open as you shop and travel to discover furnishings and elements with garden style. In addition to architectural salvage, some stores offer an interesting mix of such merchandise as cut flowers, garden tools, and vintage watering cans. Many are as pretty as they are practical.

plant blooming color indoors

74

A collection of salvaged planters offers a clear opportunity to bring the garden indoors year-round. Nestled beside a comfortable chair, these purple blossoms make an otherwise ordinary corner an enticing place to read and relax. ❏

design for **style**

75

If you leave cushions outside during warm weather, look for ones made for outdoor use, and check with fabric stores about laminating sturdy cotton for longer wear. Include pillows to brighten the look and wire plant stands to display seasonal blooms.

rooms
without walls

inviting terraces, patios, and courtyards—outdoor rooms without walls— take advantage of sun and views. Combined with porches or decks, these open spaces expand your home and garden for daily living and the possibilities of under-the-stars entertaining and dining. Often included in new construction, patios and decks adapt to most house styles and lots. Patios, a suburban staple for decades, open houses to the backyard and the outdoors. When shade is necessary because of a sunny orientation, an arbor, trellis, or fixed or retractable awning can decoratively deflect the heat of summer days.

build structures for **shade**

76

Enjoy a large deck even more with a shady, wisteria-covered arbor and an old-fashioned porch swing. Here, lush pots of mixed flowers and climbing roses transform the deck into a verdant garden retreat for relaxing and entertaining.

gather birdhouses as **garden** art

77

Assemble a tiny town of folk art birdhouses as a focal point
for your garden. When you dine alfresco, dress a picnic-style
or rustic farm table with pretty shawls, and substitute
well-worn bistro chairs for traditional benches.

combine elements through the **ages**

78

Where else could you so successfully combine a regal row of Parthenon-style bird feeders with the 1940s elegance of blossom-back metal garden chairs? The patio is the perfect place to experiment with a lighthearted mix of styles from different periods.

Collections of planted containers make the patio as lush and green as the wooded setting.

plant **flowers** in layers

79

Brighten a small deck with easy-to-plant-and-care-for pots of blooming flowers. Hang terra-cotta pots from the wall or porch ceiling for vining interest. To further this flowery mood, mix floral pattern cushions and pillows for seating comfort.

capture color with **tablecloths**

80

Turn your terrace into
an outdoor dining room
with a metal table and chair
set from a bistro or ice
cream parlor. With such
quaint pieces, you need only
a cheerful cotton cloth and
a fresh-fruit centerpiece to
welcome guests with style.

pamper in fair **weather**

81

Fair weather is your cue to bring
delicate decorating passions outdoors.
A plain cedar table becomes
sophisticated when layered with a
lavishly stitched French tablecloth. Cushy
pillows covered in pretty print fabrics
leave the living room for the afternoon
to make wooden benches comfortable.

try teatime in the **gazebo**

82

If your retreat is a gazebo, re-create the pleasures of Victorian-era outdoor teas with a decorative tablecloth, pretty table settings, and an aptly embellished teapot. Ferns hanging from the rafters recall the era when these plants were most popular.

paint your garden gate **blue**

83

Invigorate a garden or courtyard with one cheerful color. For a touch of Provence, choose French blue or rusty red as your primary hue. Finish with table linens in solids, stripes, or florals that pair with your bright accent.

A courtyard corner is a cozy sitting area with rustic natural-twig furniture, soft cushions, and plump pillows.

enjoy the **rustic** appeal of twigs

84

Emulate the romance of the forest on your terrace with colorfully cushioned and pillowed twig furniture. Look for new twig furniture at farmer's markets and in shops that carry regional crafts, or hunt for older pieces in antiques stores and vintage furniture stores. ❏

pair sporty **stripes** with pretty florals

85

Soften a woven rattan chaise with coordinating florals and awning stripes. Here, a floor lamp and petite painted table for tea complete the reading nook. Plants and a gardener's hat provide simple decorative touches.

welcome the sun

when you crave light, think "sunroom" for your family room or living room. With walls of sun-filled windows, your sitting and gathering space will be cheerful year-round. Such rooms are most comfortable with southern or eastern exposures to avoid the intense late-afternoon sun. With their technological advances, window glass or professionally applied film can block damaging sun rays. Window treatments—from shutters to blinds to shades lined with sun-resistant fabrics—stylishly guard the room from too much of a good thing.

add character with folk art

86

Look for special pieces of folk art, similar to this miniature church, or an unusual small table or two to decorate a sunroom. A painted floor and potted grass and flowers keep summer spirits alive throughout the year.

live with your **passions**

87

When you collect, focus on your favorite colors and fabrics. Botanical art and vintage vases and pots are easy-to-find collectibles that mix well with floral fabrics and architectural fragments. Group like-colored collections for impact.

employ smart **tactics** for display

88

When you're fortunate enough to have a window-wrapped room, elevate treasures to eye level and above without blocking sunlight. Here, a tole-painted tray hangs at the top of the corner window treatment, and a Victorian-era wire plant stand uplifts artwork, plants, and favorite finds without restricting the view.

make **first** impressions count

89

When your sunroom is spacious, make it a true garden room with outdoor ornaments. Shop for handsome artifacts, such as armillary spheres and weathered urns on stands, to group with reproductions or new art and accessories.

Bravely bring large-scale ornaments indoors. You'll make a grand garden style impression with just a few props.

garden **indoors** year-round

90

In this conservatory sunporch, a mini greenhouse planted with spring flowers is the colorful decorative accent. Dark wicker, dressed in green-and-white floral fabric, harmonizes with this woodsy setting.

recycle **forest** finds

91

A storm-damaged tree became fodder to furnish this garden room. To create a corner planter, the top of one log was hollowed out and filled with soil and assorted plants. Branches now serve as rustic curtain rods, and stones weight the bottoms of the fabric panels.

softly furnish a **sunroom**

92

When you spend a lot of time in your sunroom, treat it as your living room by furnishing it with comfortable upholstered pieces. Dried topiaries, in decorative urns or clay pots, impart sophisticated yet no-care touches.

play up the **theme**

93

Repeat garden motifs on several elements to emphasize
outdoor ambience. Here, a botanical-print pillow complements
the grapevine-embellished lamp base and pottery.

mix **fabrics** for easy decorating

94

Energize a white sunporch with bright and bold design elements. Tailored striped cushions, cotton pillow covers reminiscent of French country, and an upbeat lamp shade spark this scheme. Roll-up bamboo shades provide sun control.

stripe it rich

95

A sofa upholstered in bold black-and-white awning stripes stands out among this grouping of natural wicker. Summertime accessories brighten the room—even during the long, cold winter months.

Pine and wicker pair with ceramic pavers to infuse this room with warm, natural hues and textures.

bring in a garden **bench**

26

Relax a tailored white sofa with an aged garden bench
that holds drinks and displays collectibles. In one corner,
a porch balustrade is reworked as a charming vintage
birdhouse stand. ❏

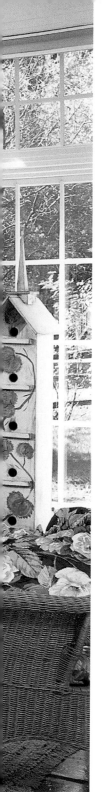

potting sheds
and tables

designed as playhouses for gardeners, potting sheds combine the practical with the aesthetic. Such structures offer places to pot, plant, prune, and nurture your plants while also serving as garden focal points. These little houses can be as simple or as elaborate as your interests, climate, and budget dictate. Inside, the plants, tools, and pots are utilitarian reminders of the garden. Depending on your needs and space, include lights, heat, or water. For admirers of garden style, these quaint hideaways lend themselves to casual retreats for meditating, sitting, dining, or entertaining like-minded souls.

create a place for everything

To organize your potting shed, shop secondhand shops and flea markets for sturdy worktables and gently worn chairs, boxes, and containers. Use the walls to hang tools and charts, both old and new, and add a drying rack to preserve the fruits of your labors.

entertain in the **garden** shed

With nods to the useful and the decorative, this garden
house welcomes workdays as well as casual, open-air
entertaining. The quirky mix of chairs and furnishings
reflects the owner's love of vintage, country style furniture.

bring **water** to your world

If space and plumbing allow, a work counter with a sink will add convenience to your potting and flower-arranging area. Here, the counter, backsplash, and shelf crafted from barn-type wood enhance the country style. Charming baskets corral the garden bounty as well as supplies.

incorporate **worn** finishes

100
Turn your back door or kitchen entry into a potting area with a dry sink or other storage piece. Look for sturdy items in distressed finishes for hints of the garden. Hang perforated hardboards or shelves to organize baskets and tools. ❏

Better Homes and Gardens® Creative Collection™

Director, Editorial Administration
Michael L. Maine

Editor-in-Chief
Beverly Rivers

Executive Editor   Karman Wittry Hotchkiss

Editorial Manager   Art Director
Ann Blevins   Don Nickell

Copy Chief	Mary Heaton
Administrative Assistant	Lori Eggers
Contributing Graphic Designer	Lauren Luftman
Contributing Copy Editor	David Kirchner

Vice President, Publishing Director
William R. Reed

Group Publisher	Steve Levinson
Senior Marketing Manager	Suzy Johnson

Chairman and CEO
William T. Kerr

In Memoriam
E. T. Meredith III (1933-2003)

Publishing Group President
Stephen M. Lacy
Magazine Group President
Jack Griffin
Publishing Group Executive Vice President
Jerry Kaplan